Charles Brockden Brown

Charles Brockden Brown

Charles Brockden Brown
American Gothic Novelist

by

HARRY R. WARFEL

OCTAGON BOOKS

A DIVISION OF FARRAR, STRAUS AND GIROUX

New York   1974

Reprinted 1974
by special arrangement with the University of Florida Press

OCTAGON BOOKS
A DIVISION OF FARRAR, STRAUS & GIROUX, INC.
19 Union Square West
New York, N. Y. 10003

Library of Congress Cataloging in Publication Data

Warfel, Harry Redcay, 1899-1971.
    Charles Brockden Brown, American Gothic novelist.

    Reprint of the ed. published by University of Florida Press,
Gainesville.

    Bibliography: p.
    1. Brown, Charles Brockden, 1771-1810.
PS1136.W3   1974   813'.2 [B]   73-19931
ISBN 0-374-98244-9

Printed in USA by
Thomson-Shore, Inc.
Dexter, Michigan

To
Mother and Dad

Preface

THIS biography tells—as fully as the scanty records permit—the life story of "the father of the American novel," who between 1798 and 1804 published seven full-length novels and fragments of several others, penned a dozen short stories, wrote much of the material in three magazines which he edited, prepared three political pamphlets, and compiled from 1806 to 1809 a semiannual cultural and historical survey of American progress in relation to world events. Although he was the most considerable man of letters in his generation, his achievement has been obscured hitherto by the lack of an accurate account of his personality and his activities. A cultural patriot with an ambition to provide the young republic with a native literature, even as Noah Webster prodded Americans to cherish a native brand of the English language, Charles Brockden Brown lived in a time when obstacles to financial success in literary enterprises were almost insurmountable. To clarify the problems he faced, I have included brief accounts of the literary, political, economic, and intellectual background. I have also made a critical analysis of each of his writings and have related his fiction to the styles and techniques popular in the 1790's in England and Germany. But major emphasis has been placed upon the presentation of every available biographical and bibliographical fact. During his lifetime he was known as Charles, and I have followed his friends' usage rather than that of recent literary his-

torians who call him Brockden. This book is the second volume—the first was Noah Webster: Schoolmaster to America *(1936)*—in a series of biographies in which I hope to explain the little-known accomplishments of relatively obscure Americans who provided inspiring intellectual leadership in this country's early national period.

Much of the information in this book is new. The only other published full-length account of Brown is William Dunlap's The Life of Charles Brockden Brown *(1815)*, a two-volume, helter-skelter, uncritical array of manuscript fragments, a few letters, and some biographical data. To the verifiable or plausibly true information given by Dunlap a century and a third ago, I have added many hitherto unpublished facts. Public records have supplied pieces of the family history, the manuscript diary of Elihu Hubbard Smith has yielded a day-to-day record of Brown's long visits to New York City from 1794 to 1798, and newspapers and magazines have furnished a record of Brown's contemporaneous reputation and accurate bibliographical evidence of his publications. From the fiction I have chosen, with due caution, a number of autobiographical passages. These sources are identified in the text or in the appended bibliographical notes, so that scholars may retrace my steps and verify the accuracy of my findings. A few words whose meanings have altered since 1810 have been glossed in square brackets, and some identifications have been indicated similarly. The punctuation, capitalization, and typography of quotations have been normalized, but otherwise the text is

Preface

as I found it. The first chapter summarizes Brown's life and achievements; the remainder of the book presents in chronological sequence the history of the family and of its distinguished son.

Carl Purrington Rollins brought to my attention, and Miss Frances G. Colt permitted me to quote from, the manuscript diary of Elihu Hubbard Smith. The Historical Society of Pennsylvania, Harvard College Library, Library of Congress, Ridgway Branch of the Philadelphia Library Company, Friends Library of Swarthmore, and the Quaker Collection in the Haverford College Library graciously permitted the use of manuscript letters in their collections. William Chadeayne, Professor and Mrs. Lewis F. Haines, J. Orin Oliphant, and William Bysshe Stein read the manuscript and put me deeply into their debt for their many helpful suggestions. It is a pleasure to express my gratitude to these persons and institutions for their friendly assistance.

HARRY R. WARFEL

University of Florida
August 17, 1949

xi

Contents

"*I Derive Pleasure from Scribbling*"

To THE political independence assured by the Treaty of Paris, Americans wanted to add cultural independence. Haltingly yet unmistakably the States ratified the Constitution and the first ten amendments, the Bill of Rights. The new freedoms required implementation. Freedom of the press would be meaningless if there were no typesetters busily imprinting a native literature in a national language. Freedom of religion would be nonexistent if foreign sectarianism draped a stifling mantle of ancient dogma upon the American soul. Just as a new political spirit created a new pattern in government, a new self-conscious intellectual spirit strove to fashion an intellectual life indigenous to and representative of a nation conceived in equalitarianism and dedicated to lofty principles of national unity founded upon individual integrity.

Charles Brockden Brown

The days of the 1770's that tried men's souls in civil strife altered in the 1790's to days that fired men's imaginations with conceptions of a limitless future glory in American action, art, learning, technology, and expression. It seems almost a truism to assert that when a group of people secures for itself a certified national boundary, or a semblance of successful government, or freedom from the yoke of subserviency, or an individuality based on a heroic past, or a linguistic unity or distinctness, it sets about energetically to achieve for itself a native art and literature. To be autochthonous, to represent the native land, to picture in word and tone and color the local as opposed to the foreign or general becomes the ideal. Americans not only fashioned such a new attitude but also discovered their unique native materials. Nature had lavished its utmost creative force in providing a background of scenic beauty, matchless fertility, and agricultural and mineral bounty. Whoever scraped a hoe in loam or bared forest earth to the sun might garner prodigal crops. In praise of so magnificent a setting only the intellectually speechless could fail to lift their voices, and only the incorrigibly perverse would twang old strings and hum the tunes of a dead past.

Where riches abound, no one man can aspire to every trophy. Nor were prizes any easier to attain in the 1790's than at any other moment. In humble, dedicated labor at congenial tasks the world's honors are won. Patiently for forty-five years Noah Webster, beginning with a shilling spelling book, laid American words together to fashion the monumental *American*

Dictionary of the English Language. Abusive epithets never deterred this lean, autumn-haired Yankee from demonstrating American linguistic independence. More quietly yet equally unwaveringly James Kent compiled *Commentaries on American Law,* a work which codified American legal decisions and replaced Blackstone as the principal sourcebook on common law. Nathaniel Bowditch set forth in *The New American Practical Navigator* the spirit of seamanship as well as the necessary mathematical formulæ. His work, like Webster's, still survives in a current revised edition. In 1798 Eli Whitney, perfecter of the cotton gin, demonstrated the principle of interchangeable parts, an important stimulus to American technological development. Each of these men of humble beginning, together with the molders in the 1790's of the political state—Washington, Jefferson, Hamilton, and John Adams—has left an abiding legacy of universally applicable principles based upon a first-hand examination of his immediate environment.

If Webster, Kent, Bowditch, Whitney, Washington, Jefferson, Hamilton, and Adams rose like mountain peaks above other patriots in the 1790's, they towered not like lonely spires. Research and writing were carried on in almost every field of learning. Through books, orations, and personal example many men and women gave stimulus to intellectual activities in the United States; even if their offerings fell short of genius, their unceasing labor made possible the greater work of others in a later generation. Many trees create a forest; the tallest and straightest to a degree owe their height and erectness to their smaller companions.

Not least among these others, a frail, short-lived tree in the forest, was Charles Brockden Brown, a Philadelphian of Quaker descent. Four melodramatic terror novels, one of them—*Wieland* (1798)—a minor classic in American literature, have earned him the somewhat fanciful title of "father of the American novel." The other three novels are *Ormond*, *Edgar Huntly*, and *Arthur Mervyn*. His work anticipated Poe's and Hawthorne's in subject, style, mood, and intellectual elevation; these later masters referred in friendly terms to the pioneer's work. As late as 1845 in "P's Correspondence," Hawthorne stated that "no American writer enjoys a more classic reputation."

In the long arid years before James Fenimore Cooper in *The Spy* (1821) proved that an American could write vivid fiction, Brown's writings had given promise that Americans could compete successfully with transatlantic novelists and could utilize native scenery effectively. Every cultural patriot had echoed Noah Webster's cry: "America must be as independent in *literature* as she is in *politics*—as famous for *arts* as for *arms*." By comparison with the youthful aspirants for literary honors at Harvard, Yale, and Princeton, where epic poems and Addisonian essays had been planned and seldom written, Brown in his brief day seemed to be the answer to American prayers for a native literary genius. Avowedly he wrote from an American point of view about recent occurrences in the United States. Nationalistically he deemed transatlantic systems of ethics inapplicable to America, and as a critic he issued a call for books and magazines informed with American concepts of liberty, equality, and religious toleration.

Pleasure from Scribbling

Brown's merits as a novelist are substantial. Contemporary story patterns, especially the seduction motif essential to every eighteenth-century novel and play, were molded into new shapes and then subtly universalized by subordinating melodramatic action to psychological probing into the springs of abnormal conduct. No other writer before Poe traced so carefully or illustrated so well the strange manifestations of obsessions and perversity. Just as Dr. Benjamin Rush studied mental diseases in the University of Pennsylvania Hospital, so Brown deftly bared strange physical responses observable in delusion and hysteria.

In modifying contemporaneous English and German patterns to fit his own theory of fiction, Brown adopted the Gothic formula of murder and midnight seduction for achieving effects of terror and horror, but he rejected familiar castle trappings and placed his stories in ordinary houses in American settings. Instead of ghosts and other supernatural or pseudo-supernatural manifestations, he used the wonders of nature and of human power which seem supernatural to the inexpert observer. Some of these, which were described in medical treatises, were ventriloquism, spontaneous combustion of the human body, identity of fate in twins, religious mania, homosexuality, and sleepwalking. Each incident had its counterpart in reported experience, so that while adhering to the principle of basing stories on fact, he could fulfill an ambition to "excite and baffle curiosity without shocking belief."

Early in his career Brown called himself a "storytelling moralist." Narrative was incidental to truth; consequently his failure in fiction arose chiefly from emphasizing ideas and piling undeveloped incident upon incident. Seldom was an episode expanded to its fullest possibilities through conversation and description. Narrative emerged through expository summary, highlighted with brilliantly phrased maxims. Occasional attempts at dialect—Negro, German, and Irish— indicated an awareness of fiction's direction in becoming a careful transcript of daily experience. Though a series of remarkable events sought "to enchain the reader's interest," ideas always remained of primary importance.

A child of the Enlightenment, Brown conceived of fiction as a means of enforcing wholesome lessons. Just as Addison had "brought philosophy out of closets and libraries, schools and colleges, to dwell in clubs and assemblies, at tea tables and in coffee houses," so this American novelist wished his writings to clarify the springs of human action and to give wholesome interpretations of the duties required of men and women in a rational world. In his estimation an author is duty-bound to "render counsel palatable" by demonstrating "ingenuous candor and unaffected benignity," to be sincere, to avoid skepticism, to "possess a competent knowledge of the human heart, its windings and labyrinths," and to delineate "American opinions and customs" with patriotic fervor. This critical creed stemmed from, even as it abetted, cultural nationalism in the young nation.

Sensitive, precocious, and studious, young Brown early conceived the notion that ideas guide society, that most worthy of acclaim is he who directs the nation in correct ethical courses, and that of all writers the moralist is the most useful. "I reflected," he wrote, "that the source of all energy, even of life, is seated in thought." His reading, therefore, consisted of a search for generalizations likely to expand his knowledge of human behavior. "What insight may be gained," he declared, "into the mechanism of human society and the laws of human action by pursuing the vicissitudes of individuals or of nations from their hour of birth to their hour of extinction!"

Brown's earliest writings ally him with the liberalism of William Godwin, and it has been asserted that Brown owed most of his political ideas to this English thinker. Godwin's influence on Brown was immense, especially in providing a pattern of rationalistic social thought by which to test opinions and experience. Yet the seeds of liberalism were in the age and not only in *An Enquiry into Political Justice.*

From the beginning Brown took his intellectual direction from the liberal thinking of the Friends. He enunciated broad humanitarian concepts: It is incumbent upon a generous-minded person to hate war and dueling, to support the antislavery movement, to ameliorate the plight of the underprivileged, to strive for social justice, and to strike off ancient fetters abridging human freedom. In propagating general notions of social virtue, personal integrity, and religious tolerance, he leaned to the deistic view. His rationalistic religion stressed belief in God and the cultivation through reason of the social and civic duties. The Church as an institution, as well as metaphysical, hair-splitting doctrinal disputation, consumed little of his energy.

The outstanding contribution to fiction of this Quaker novelist is not his ideas nor his Gothicism, but his psychological probing into the minds of people under various kinds of tension. Believing that "human life abounds in mysterious appearances" and that the mind has only its perceptions to prepare its judgments, he adopted a rationalistic, inquisitive attitude toward mental phenomena. Most of his fully developed fictional characters possess phobias or manias or biases traceable to some childhood experience, unfortunate environmental circumstance, or hereditary tendency. Nearly all are introverts who freely discuss their weaknesses.

In spite of his factual sources and his psychological analysis of character, Brown was essentially a bookish person deriving his knowledge of the universe from the printed page and not from nature. At every opportunity he hid in a corner with a book or sat at a writing table. Books could comfort or enrage him; life, seldom. Existence, he complained, was a continuous dull ache. Shortly before death he remarked that he could not recall a single day free from pain. Morbid depression and melancholy clouded his spirit. Physical frailty—gastric trouble combined with incipient tuberculosis—seemed the harsh lot assigned by fate. Normal social pleasures were impossible for long periods. Excursions to recover his health usually aggravated his distress; he heard only his throbbing nerves, and the smiling aspects of nature hid behind the dark veil of melancholy.

Some relief from pain came from conversation. As soon as a friend started a topic, Brown prattled endlessly, not so much pleased at his eloquence as relieved from bodily aches. In his clubs he either took a leading part or withdrew. James Kent once reprimanded him for usurping too much time at the Friendly Club.

Reading similarly gave surcease from sorrow. Books were companions on every journey. He read through the encyclopedia; he held memberships in libraries; and he acquired a large personal library. Milton early became a favorite poet; Shakespeare was systematically reread; and the current magazines and newspapers were conned with scholarly care. Robert Proud taught him to cherish the Latin of Cicero; he learned French alone, and at the age of thirty he studied German. Although he read nearly all available fiction, he gave preference to serious tomes as alone worthy of a rational mind.

"The pen is the pacifier," Brown declared in *Arthur Mervyn*. "It checks the mind's career; it circumscribes her wanderings. It traces out and compels us to adhere to one path. It ever was my friend. Often it has blunted my vexations, hushed my stormy passions, turned my peevishness to soothing, my fierce revenge to heart-dissolving pity." At another time he wrote: "I derive pleasure from scribbling thus. It is a mental recreation more salutary to the jaded spirits than a ramble in the fields or a contemplation of the starry heavens. I like it better than walking and conversing with my only friend, but there is time enough for both to be done." Writing was a therapeutic agent as well as an art; in producing a useful medicinal effect upon the author, an essay or story served its purpose.

Brown renounced his career in fiction after 1801 at the behest of his brothers. He joined them in a shipping business, the profits of which for a time were large, but the urge to write remained with him. In 1803 he allied himself with a firm of printers, edited a magazine, did translating, wrote political pamphlets against Jefferson, planned a large geography of the world, and, as he neared the end of his short life, compiled a semiannual *American Register*. In these works he was no less forceful as a moralist—and probably more useful to his fellows—than as a novelist; certainly the public paid more liberally for these hack performances than for minor fictional classics. One pamphlet on the Louisiana Territory created a political sensation; it was reprinted and discussed as thoroughly as if it had been a presidential utterance. A hitherto unrewarded novelist could not but congratulate himself upon his new importance in the literary world.

In appearance Brown was "short and dumpy, with light eyes, and hair inclining to be sandy, while the expression of his face reflected ill health rather than intellect. The lines on his brow seemed to have been corroded by consumption, not chiseled by midnight meditations. A weak constitution had been his parents' legacy to him. Yet vividly in his countenance glowed the light of benevolence." In young manhood Brown was a cheerful, often an entertaining, companion. His conversation, when animated by a worthy subject, scintillated. Yet he often sat brooding upon his luckless state. When asked by John Bernard to explain how a man so full of cheer could write somber stories, Brown replied:

I am conscious of a double mental existence. When I am sufficiently excited to write, all my ideas flow naturally and irresistibly through the medium of sympathies which steep them in shade, though the feelings they bring are so pleasing as to prevent my perceiving it. The tone of my works being thus the necessary result of the advancement of those truths or discoveries which lead me to composition, I am made so happy by it for the time as to be ignorant of its real effect upon my reader. This I term, therefore, my imaginative being. My social one has more of light than darkness upon it, because, unless I could carry into society the excitement which makes me write, I could not fall into its feelings. Perhaps the difference of the two may be thus summed up: in my literary moods I am aiming at making the world something better than I find it; in my social ones I am content to take it as it is.

Brown's great ambition, like that of Poe thirty years later, was to create, through the medium of magazines, an American literary public sympathetic to and willing to support native authors. This effort failed, partly because of Brown's shortcomings and partly because of insurmountable obstacles inherent in America's social structure. Materially America had greatly improved in the twenty years following the close of the Revolution. The new century offered every indication of future greatness; the present, however, remained esthetically bleak and barren. Business, agriculture, and politics occupied men's attention. The embargo and nonintercourse acts of Jefferson threw business into a state of distrust approaching panic. Schools were still inadequate; colleges were poorly supported and attended. The cultural level of the nation had risen but slightly since 1700; a nation-wide audience for poets and novelists had not developed. America was still a frontier nation. In the cities alone lay a hope of artistic and cultural progress. The countryside, increasingly settled by immigrant farmers, gave almost no encouragement to artistic endeavor. Evangelical revivals reawakened fears against devil-sponsored novels, plays, dancing, and the theater. Traffic in liberal ideas rendered an author suspect. The times, indeed, were unfavorable; only American textbook and handbook writers produced works to vie successfully with the books imported from England or to win the attention of a nation whose chief reading matter was the newspaper.

In himself, Brown lacked the qualities which would have made for popular success in such a time. Energy and devotion he possessed, but literary training and control he did not have. Humor he lacked utterly, and, unlike Hugh Henry Brackenridge, he could not win readers by laughter as well as soberness. Frontier people, it seems, must laugh to live. They are willing to laugh at themselves or at others, but laugh they must. Nor could Brown succeed in giving dramatic surge to recent or contemporary materials suitable for romance. Overburdened with thought, he failed to see opportunities for portraying ordinary human experience; he preferred terror, melodrama, and abnormality. As a critic and editor he lacked Dennie's clear perception of the popular literary taste of his time.

And yet the influence of Brown was good. He strove to place America on a par with European nations in literary matters. He dissented from the current opinion that poor native products deserve praise merely because they are native. He insisted upon the validity of local materials in the development of an American literature. He brought Americans face to face with the need for adequate national self-expression. Few men could have done more, and if he seems to have failed, his victory in spite of defeat is the greater because of the isolated excellence of his fiction and because of his spirited insistence upon American literary self-reliance.

Substantial Quaker Stock

CHARLES BROCKDEN BROWN was born in Philadelphia on January 17, 1771, the son of Elijah and Mary Armitt Brown. Although in manhood the novelist frequently complained that the register of famous names never included one representative of his family, worthy Quaker blood coursed through the veins of the Browns and Armitts. From generation to generation there had descended a heritage of active endeavor coupled with a tolerant interest in liberal ideas.

This branch of the Brown family was established in America in 1677 by James Browne, who with other newcomers laid out the town of Burlington, New Jersey. Browne had left England in the ship *Kent* to escape the abuse showered upon simple nonconformist plain people. Forbidden to gather in meeting houses in England, the Quakers had assembled to worship in the streets. For more than a year before their departure they were abused by bands of taunters and by the soldiery. On one occasion bullies broke up a meeting and pummeled the worshipers. At another time hot coals and popping firecrackers were tossed upon them from second-story windows. At still another time a shower of excrement cascaded on the bowed heads of the group. When the exhorter Richard Samble was found on his knees, he was hustled to court and fined for being a preacher.

James Browne, the pioneer, was the fourth son of Richard and Mary Browne of Sywell, Northamptonshire, a couple who were converted to Quakerism shortly after James' birth on March 26, 1656. To live in a settlement with Quaker sympathies, they moved to Paddington, Bedfordshire. On September 28, 1662, Richard died. How the widow supported herself and her son is not known. At the age of twenty-one James joined the colonists. Apparently he remained at Burlington only a short time, for in 1678 his name is listed among the settlers at Chichester, now Marcus Hook, Pennsylvania. On June 8, 1679, in the primitive meeting house at Burlington he and Honour Clayton, a fellow passenger on the *Kent*, were married. It was the first marriage recorded in New Jersey. James and Honour lived on the place, "Podington," on Chichester Creek until 1705, when the property was deeded to their son William. James moved "into the wilderness" at Nottingham, Pennsylvania, where he died in 1716.

James' son William was born on January 13, 1682. Following his marriage to Esther Yardley of Bucks County, Pennsylvania, he moved to Maryland. Here was born to William and Esther as their third child and second son, James, the grandfather of the novelist. Extant records contain little more than vital statistics, so that details of the activities of William and James are not known. At East Nottingham on October 4, 1734, James married Miriam Churchman. Five children were born to this couple: Edward in 1735, Hannah in 1737, Elijah, to become the father of the novelist, on March 12, 1740, Estor in 1742, and William in 1746.

Elijah Brown at about the age of twelve studied in the Friends' Grammar School in Philadelphia. At seventeen, on February 19, 1757, while still an apprentice, he received a certificate of dismissal from East Nottingham to the Philadelphia meeting: "He has been a dutiful child to his parents, soberly inclined, and of a good repute amongst us according to his age." On July 9, 1761, in the Arch Street Meeting House, Philadelphia, he married Mary Armitt, the daughter of the late Joseph Armitt and Elizabeth Lisle Armitt. Elizabeth was a daughter of Maurice Lisle and a granddaughter of Henry Badcock, a wealthy brewer. The Armitts had amassed a considerable fortune; Mrs. Elizabeth Armitt's name appears frequently in Philadelphia land records in the purchase and sale of real estate. The newlyweds made their home with Mrs. Armitt at 117 South Second Street; here were born their six children: Joseph Armitt Brown, who in the midst of a successful career as merchant importer died on October 29, 1807, at Flushing in Holland; James, Armitt, and Elijah, Jr., who became merchants; Charles Brockden; and Elizabeth Armitt, who was married to Stacy Horner on November 30, 1797.

Elijah Brown's career as a conveyancer was fitted to the circumstances of his marriage. His work consisted in the writing of deeds, leases, and other legal documents transferring real estate from one person to another; he served as broker in real estate and mortgage transactions, and he managed real estate and other investments for widows and estates. Doubtless a fair share of this activity centered in protecting the interests of his mother-in-law, Mrs. Armitt, and other relatives. In 1785 the Philadelphia Directory listed him in this occupation with an office in the rear of St. Paul's Church on Pear Street, between Third and Dock streets. This building still (1949) stands at 216 Chancellor Street. A journal survives for the years 1794-1797. In it are listed properties for rent or sale, money available for mortgages, and similar items of business information.

Among the entries in Elijah Brown's journal are extracts from books he had recently read. These books include William Godwin's *An Enquiry into Political Justice*, Mary Wollstonecraft's *An Historical and Moral View of the French Revolution* (this volume had been purchased as a present for Elijah, Jr.), Helen Maria Williams' *Letters on the War in France*, Epictetus' *Morals*, Job Scott's *Journal*, and Robert Bage's novel *Man as He Is*, from which was copied a favorable picture of English Quakers. Here, too, carefully engrossed, is "A Confession of Faith, Containing Twenty-three Articles, of the People Called Quakers." This reading reflected an interest in the liberal ideas being presented in current literature, as well as a concern for an accurate knowledge of the experiences and beliefs of his sect.

Elijah's eldest son, Joseph Armitt Brown, voyaged frequently to the West Indies, Europe, and the Near East from his headquarters in Edenton, North Carolina. His wealth was such that the will of his mother, opened after her death in 1825, left no part of her property directly to his children, since ample provision for them had been made from his estate in 1807. On his return from trading trips Joseph doubtless brought, together with merchantable goods, many books and rich talk about foreign lands, people, and customs. Elijah, Jr., Armitt, and James similarly traveled extensively and always manifested an interest in books. In this well-to-do home, crammed with books and maps and echoing with current liberal thought as recorded in essays and novels, Charles Brockden Brown's decision to attempt a literary career probably did not seem strange, nor the ambition unworthy.

Elijah Brown's awareness of the radical doctrines of contemporary writers in no wise dimmed his Quaker ardor. Frowned upon was the tendency to relax standards once maintained in spite of bitter persecution. The customs of these chosen people were firmly believed to be right. Brown gathered his children about him to discuss the problems facing each one as a citizen and as a Christian. Occasionally older members of the Meeting reviewed with them the grounds of their faith. In their view, God endowed every human being with a measure of His own Divine Spirit. Within each person is the Inner Light of Christ. A life in conformity with the will of the Heavenly Father will result in the application of the principle of love to the whole of life. "The immanence of God implies the sonship

stamped along with the aid of a silver-headed cane. Wise, calm, mild, energetic, resourceful, affectionate, he was the living embodiment of the Quaker philosophy. Aware of the ways of the world, he guided his pupils into suitable vocational activities.

As a lad, Charles devoured books as other children relish candy. The facts of geography slipped into orderly array as his brothers reported upon voyages or itineraries of trading vessels in which they held investments. The family used the globe and atlas as commonplace tools. On the parlor bookshelf rested fat calfskin volumes by travelers and merchant explorers, whose strange tales of adventure supplied engrossing background information for the lad as well as for those who interpreted trade reports published in European periodicals and American newspapers. At the age of ten Charles remonstrated when a stranger called him *boy:* "Why does he call me boy? Does he not know that it is neither size nor age but understanding that makes the man? I could ask him an hundred questions, none of which he could answer!" Every youth occasionally feels this burst of indignation, for what lad does not think himself the possessor of information about the odd quirks of humanity and of nature which sages never scribbled into learned tomes.

This devotion to books resulted partly from the infirm state of the boy's health. A slender frame housed a delicate constitution. Prospects of a healthy manhood were doubtful; the family, anxious to fulfill the frail boy's wishes, allowed him to follow his whims. While other lads played games or worked as apprentices in offices, stores, mills, or on sailing vessels, Charles hugged a book close by a window facing Second Street. Grandmother Armitt, fondly standing guard, shielded him from the rude boisterousness of sturdy boys. Only Robert Proud discerned the flaw and counseled against this abnormal thralldom to books; he urged the lad to walk in the woods and to strengthen his body by regular, easy exercise. Though Charles wandered along the river bank and occasionally searched the thickets for blackberries and grapes, he never relaxed his thoughtful activities nor substituted natural lore for the abstractions of books.

"I sought not the society of persons of my own age," he said autobiographically in *ArthurMervyn*, "not from sullen or unsociable habits, but merely because those around me were totally unlike myself. Their tastes and occupations were incompatible with mine. In my few books, in my pen, in the vegetable and animal existences around me, I found companions who adapted their visits and intercourse to my convenience and caprice, and with whom I was never tired of communing." In another autobiographical passage Brown wrote: "I scarcely know how to convey to you just ideas of so motley a character as mine was in my juvenile days. I was the slave of fantasies and contradictions. My preceptors were books. These were of such a kind as to make me wise in speculation but absurd in practice. I had blended the illusions of poetry with the essences of science [factual knowledge]. My mind was fertile in reasoning and invention, and my theory was not incorrect; but my practical notions of happiness and dignity were full of imbecility and folly."

When he left Robert Proud's school in 1786 or

1787, Charles' moral and intellectual course had been charted. "When the appetites are vigorous, the senses keen, and the conduct regulated by temper and passion [that is, temperament and emotion], rather than by prudence and experience," Brown wrote, "we are most alive to all impressions, and generally take that path which we pursue for the rest of our days." This path was not a paved highway to professional success, but a winding lane darkened by melancholy shadows of poor health. During brief periods of sunlight he trudged vigorously toward eminence in literature. He had already become a tolerable Latin scholar; he had versified portions of Job, the Psalms, and Ossian; he had written essays and original verses; and, to join Dwight, Barlow, Freneau, and the ever-brightening galaxy of epic poets in the literary firmament, he had planned epic poems on Columbus' discovery of America, Pizarro's conquest of Peru, and Cortez' expedition into Mexico. None of this early work survives.

Family membership in the Library Company of Philadelphia made possible wide, if not wise, excursions through the realms of print. From circulating libraries he borrowed books and periodicals freshly imported from London and Dublin. Especially interesting were publications dealing with architecture, possibly because of the family's financial interest in the building boom in Philadelphia. He invented a type of shorthand for his own use, and he studied French without a tutor. It remains a matter of doubt whether he had learned by this time the language of the Germans making up one third of the population in and near Philadelphia, some of whom must have been his schoolfellows or friends.

Into a journal and in straggling letters to his companions, Charles, self-consciously disburdening his mind of new-found wisdom, began to draw the outline of a new Utopia, a young Quaker revolutionist's panacea for the world's ills. In 1787, the year of the Constitutional Convention, liberal Americans planned to remodel their government and to establish a code of human conduct expressive of a belief in human perfectibility. With eager breath Charles sucked in every new doctrine likely to emancipate mankind from old fetters. At home and at Weekly Meeting the talk was rich in allusions to bright dreams for attaining a New Jerusalem on this earth. The Friends had established their colony and their city upon terms of brotherly love; they had lived for more than a century without a single misunderstanding with the Indians. Utopian notions seemed feasible in the light of the Friends' successful practice of the Christian principle of brotherhood. Had not Anthony Benezet preached antislavery doctrines among willing listeners in the Society of Friends? Had not John Woolman demonstrated the beauty of a life devoted to self-sacrifice? Had not the movement for penal reform originated in Philadelphia? Had not the public care of insane people been undertaken in Philadelphia? Was it not a belief of the Quakers that every man, however sinful, might be regenerated by the Inner Light of Christ? Had not the Quakers permitted an equality between male and female beyond that admitted in other sects? The Quakers had been the radicals of the seventeenth century; although some of their descendants by the end of the next century had grown toughly conservative, such men as Elijah Brown still kept their minds open to new, uplifting, humanitarian thoughts. In the books of Rousseau, of Richard Price, and possibly of the German sentimentalists, as well as of other men who had left the beaten path of orthodox theology, Charles found support for his ideas. The wonder is not that he started on the path of radical social philosophizing, but that, with his feverish temper, he did not journey further until he reached a lonely eminence like that of Thomas Paine or William Godwin.

Unhappy Law Student

AFTER completing the course at Latin School, Charles did not enter the University of Pennsylvania, for he possessed the quite common Quaker contempt for college training. "We were saved," he said in *Wieland*, "from the corruption and tyranny of college and boarding schools." He read law in the Arch Street office of Alexander Willcocks, an urbane gentleman and accomplished legal scholar with a reputation for strict impartiality and inflexible integrity. In the United States the law then led more effectually and more directly to advancement than any other profession. Because of lucrative rewards, many young men with fathers well established in business or politics studied Blackstone as the surest means of building up a name or a fortune.

Family wishes probably influenced Brown's choice of a profession. While the robust brothers engaged in trade, the frail booklover could untangle legal knots in which the businessmen unwittingly might be snared. For a time there were reports of assiduous application to duty. As a member of the Legal Society where he sat in judgment upon disputants, he wrote cool, unadorned decisions, some of which are printed in Dunlap's biography of Brown. From 1789 to 1791, when Willcocks served as City Recorder, Charles doubtless spent many hours daily as a mere copyist, repeatedly inditing identical legal papers, such as deeds, quitclaims, ground rents, and contracts. A young man with three epic poems swirling in his brain soon grows despondent if every long sheet of white paper is to be filled, not with bright poetic originality, but with centuries-old phrases drawn from English common law.

Musty indeed was the law. "The task assigned [me] was technical and formal," he complained. "[I] was perpetually encumbered with the rubbish of law, and waded with laborious steps through its endless tautologies, its impertinent circuities, its lying assertions and hateful artifices. Nothing occurred to relieve or diversify the scene. It was one tedious round of scrawling and jargon, a tissue made up of the shreds and remnants of barbarous antiquity, polluted with the rust of ages, and patched by the stupidity of modern workmen into new deformity."

Jaded spirits followed each day's reluctant application to the study of Blackstone and Coke: "I find vigorous efforts are necessary to keep my attention from straying from a page, which seems to me replete with frivolous subtleties and injurious distinctions. When my task is finished with the day, it leaves me listless and melancholy. I perceive that I have retained little of the day's reading, and am haunted by a kind of pre-sentiment that what is wearisome today will be still more so tomorrow, and will at length become insupport-able. Overpowered with fatigue, I am prompted to seek relief in walking, and my mind, untuned and destitute of energy, is lost in a dreary confusion of images."

On leaving Willcocks' office each evening, Charles went to his room to scribble comments on the day's events or to write letters. A youth named Davidson invited Charles to become a member of the Belles Lettres Society, a club designed to improve its nine members in composition and public speaking. An early hesitancy soon altered to enthusiasm which carried him to leadership. At the first meeting Charles delivered an address upon the objects of the society; it was a desultory, high-flown exhortation to his fellows "to ornament the mind as well as to improve the understanding." Later he discoursed on "the relation, dependence, and connection of the several parts of knowledge." This brief summation of vast volumes of learning contained generalizations rather than precise factual information; descriptive artistry did not sharpen the outlines of somewhat nebulous concepts. To the end of his career these weaknesses flawed Brown's writing.

Among Charles' friends in the Belles Lettres Society were William Wood Wilkins, Timothy Paxson, Joseph Bringhurst, Jr., Zachariah Poulson, Jr., Peter Thompson, and Thomas P. Cope. Wilkins, a law student from Gloucester, New Jersey, carried messages between Willcocks and John Todd, Wilkins' employer. For many months Wilkins had remained friendless in the city; unwearied diligence in pursuing legal studies had exhausted his bodily and mental strength. His light-heartedness shifted to complaints of depression of spirits. He sat down indifferent to books, discontented with himself, overpowered by a painful lassitude for which his inexperience could find no cause. At this juncture, on July 6, 1789, Brown introduced Wilkins to the society; the new member at once reoriented his life to make provision for social and intellectual diversion.

Brown and Wilkins were similar in physical frailty, in literary ambition, and in a tendency to subside too readily into melancholy. They became confidants, each unbosoming himself unrestrainedly in long letters until Wilkins' death in 1795. Although the eighteenth century saw the rise of a cult of graveyard poetry fostering a sober-suited mood, it was in no dilettante pose that these youths penned thoughts of self-annihilation. Partly because of illness and partly because of increasing dissatisfaction with the law as a profession, Brown told Wilkins: "Had I never had friends and relations, I am convinced that before this time I had ceased either to exist, or to exist as an inhabitant of America." Suicide or escape to a distant land is a familiar psychological signal. Clinging to each other in stormy moments, these lads managed to retain buoyancy.

During 1789 some of Brown's scribblings found their way into print. His earliest unmistakably identified composition comprises four quatrains, "An Inscription for General Washington's Tombstone." The verse itself has no merit, but an amusing anecdote is related about it by Dunlap:

[*31*]

About this time he published in an Edenton news-paper a poetical address to Dr. Franklin. "The blundering printer," says Charles in his journal, "from his zeal or his ignorance, or perhaps from both, substituted the name of Washington. Washington therefore stands arrayed in awkward colors. Philosophy smiles to behold her darling son; she turns with horror and disgust from those who have won the laurel of victory in the field of battle, to this her favorite candidate who had never participated in such bloody glory, and whose fame was derived from the conquest of philosophy alone. The printer by his blundering ingenuity made the subject ridiculous. Every word of this clumsy panegyric was a direct slander upon Washington, and so it was regarded at the time."

Joseph Armitt Brown doubtless carried the verses with him on one of his journeys to Edenton, where he exhibited them with fraternal pride to Hodge and Wills, the publishers of *The State Gazette of North Carolina*, who took a copy for their weekly. How and why Franklin's name was replaced by Washington's we cannot know; a plausible guess would be that the impending inauguration of Washington as first President of the United States demanded a patriotic poem, and, lacking other suitable materials, the editor resorted to the simple expedient of turning the soldier into a philosopher. The verse appeared on February 26, 1789:

> *The shade of great Newton shall mourn,*
> *And yield him Philosophy's throne;*
> *The palm from her brow shall be torn,*
> *And given to Washington alone.*

Unhappy Law Student

His brows ever shall be adorn'd
  With laurels that never decay;
His laws mighty nations unborn
  And ages remote shall obey.

Him liberty crown'd with her wreath;
  Philosophy shew'd him her plan,
Whilst the Muses inscrib'd underneath
  The hero, the sage, and the man.

Let candour then write on his tomb:
  Here America's favorite lies,
Whose soul, for the want of due room,
  Has left us to range in the skies.

In August, 1789, the Philadelphia *Columbian Magazine* published a series of periodical papers under the name "The Rhapsodist." The editor greeted the fledgling contributor eagerly: "We thank the Rhapsodist and solicit the continuation of his essays." These were signed in succession by the letters: B, R, O, W. Because the *Columbian* paid for contributions, its pages contain some of the best writing produced in the young republic. In imitation of Addison and Steele's *Spectator*, "The Rhapsodist" contains a central character whose leading traits invite general interest. In promising to tell the truth about himself the young author began his career with a solemnity destined always to mark his writing:

I speak seriously when I affirm that no situation whatsoever will justify a man in uttering a falsehood. . . . I have been told that my opinions respecting this subject are singular. . . . Truth is with me the test of every man's character. Wherever I perceive the least inclination to deceive, I suspect a growing depravity of soul that will one day be productive of the most dangerous consequences. Falsehood and dissimulation, however embellished with the softest colors and touched by the most sparing and delicate hand, stamp an infamy upon the character hardly to be equaled by the perpetration of the blackest crimes. . . . I am . . . careful to regulate my own conduct by the immutable standard. My scruples in this respect have been ridiculed by my friends as absurd and extravagant.

Brown defines a rhapsodist as "one who delivers the sentiments suggested by the moment in artless and unpremeditated language. . . . He pours forth the effusions of a sprightly fancy, and describes the devious wanderings of a quick but thoughtful mind. But he is equally remote from the giddy raptures of enthusiasm and the sober didactic strains of dull philosophy." The youthful author, while denying that he is painting a self-portrait, yet adheres closely to his idealistic dreams. He strains after perfection by seeking mystic communion in nature, where his imagination "peoples every object with ideal beings, and the barrier between himself and the world of spirits seems burst by the force of meditation." In this solitude he found his most satisfying companionship. After months spent alone in an Ohio wilderness, where the rhapsodist "contemplated the fabric of human nature as it appears in a book," he returned to society. Strange sensations made him feel "how unavailing is knowledge unless it is derived from experience," and how necessary it is to "consent to live according to the forms of polished life."

Unhappy Law Student

Unable to sustain the rhapsodical character type, Brown lapsed in the fourth essay into a turgid account of an entanglement occasioned by the intrusion of a correspondent. So pointless was this essay that the editors, once so jubilant over their contributor's ability, refused to accept further pieces. Yet in these essays are hints of the novelist to come. A moralist is coining maxims for the guidance of society, and these are presented semiautobiographically. Allusions to the Ohio country, to a wilderness retreat, and to Cicero recur in the novels. Narrative begins to elbow its way into the exposition. At no time in his career does Brown really master the technique of fiction or of exposition; these halting first compositions indicate why it took nine years of painful struggle to find a satisfactory medium for ideas struggling for expression.

In 1790 Charles participated in the formation of the Society for the Attainment of Useful Knowledge, an organization modeled somewhat on its predecessors, the Legal Society and the Belles Lettres Society. Debates were held on such topics as "Is Suicide Justifiable?" and "Are Speculations in the Public Funds Injurious?" Brown remained a member as late as 1796; none of his writings for this society has been identified.

Actively increasing his circle of acquaintances, he almost daily called upon friends and relatives. In his remaining free hours he journalized, composed letters, or wrote poems and essays. Yet his mind remained clouded in a mood of Wertherism, of world-weariness so common in the late eighteenth century. His diary and letters for this period, it is said, "read like pages from the *Journal* of Amiel, in the aversion to an active life, the love of self-analysis, and the faculty of morbid philosophizing." This self-pitying vein remained in Brown's letters until his marriage in 1804. Yet in social intercourse he was bright, cheerful, argumentative, forceful, seldom giving evidence of the blue devils which goaded his mind to suicidal thoughts.

Among Brown's papers printed in Dunlap's *Life* were letters to and from Henrietta G., a very beautiful New England maiden whom the author wooed passionately and unsuccessfully. The correspondence flows along like that of a typical epistolary romance; doubtless an interest in fiction had already led Brown to try his hand at this form of composition. Whether or not a love affair unsettled his serenity, the youngster had sufficient cause for unhappiness.

An increasing detestation for the dull prolixities of the law gnawed at Brown's mind. Attempts were made to cheer him with the thought that a right attitude would come with the unfolding to his understanding of the principles of law. His answer was that he could not learn the law "in this theater of noise, jarring, stunning, monotonous; this concourse of cold hearts and busy faces; this receptacle of squalid and gaudy misery, of noisome plague-begetting smells." Only by an act of the will, he confessed, could his mind be kept on his work.

Shortly after his twenty-first birthday in 1792, Brown resigned from Willcocks' law office and never once thereafter uttered a sentence regretting the decision. At home his action was justified in long soliloquies; "he resorted," says Dunlap, "to all the sophisms and paradoxes with which ignorance and ingenious prejudice had assailed the science or the practice of law. He professed that he could not reconcile it with his ideas of morality to become indiscriminately the defender of right or wrong." He refused to champion injustice, to become the auxiliary in the cause of wrong, or to suffer remorse of conscience merely for the sake of achieving notoriety and wealth. Dunlap assumed that the decision resulted from qualities described in "The Rhapsodist," a love of solitude and a shrinking from society with its frivolous chat arising from folly, ignorance, and cupidity.

The wavering in his professional intentions occurred not merely because he had glimpsed more enticing areas in a dream world, but for other reasons. For one thing, his health again declined. Continuous sedentary labor doubtless had brought on fitful coughing spells and gastric pains. The family, too well aware of their favorite's fragility, counseled at first a less drastic step than resignation of professional opportunities, but soon a pained silence greeted his excuses. The subject was taboo, though it always hung in midair ready to be clanged like a bell as a reminder of his apostasy. Once again his elders unbridled the young colt, allowing him free rein to follow his literary inclination. They were the more willing because Charles had fallen into a savagely melancholy mood. Life had grown meaningless. Disease threatened to end his career on its very threshold. Love, too, was inflicting harsh wounds on the sensitive youth. He wandered aimlessly through the surrounding woods, tramping along the Wissahickon Creek, along the Schuylkill and Delaware rivers, where the views supposedly matched Europe's fabled scenery.

With trepidation the family awaited his return each day. His health slowly improved; with reviving vigor came better spirits and the desire to live.

Charles had abandoned the law, too, because inner compulsions drove him into more congenial activities. At this time he lacked power of concentration on tasks requiring detailed analysis; he possessed no interest in, nor could he secure satisfaction from, mathematical and scientific investigation. Although he wandered through the fields, he never brought home a flower, a leaf, a feather, or a stone as a specimen. Unlike most lads, he never made a collection of natural objects. He simply had no capacity for close observation. "If men be chiefly distinguished from each other," he says, "by the modes in which attention is employed, either on external and sensible objects, or merely on abstract ideas and the creatures of reflection, I may justly claim to be enrolled in the second class. My existence is a series of thoughts rather than of motions. Ratiocination and deduction leave my senses unemployed. The fullness of my fancy renders my eye vacant and inactive. Sensations do not precede and suggest, but follow and are secondary to the acts of my mind." As a result of this mental tendency Brown's letters describing journeys through picturesque sections of Pennsylvania, New Jersey, and New York are phrased in unperceptive, generalized language. Love of nature, a necessary sentiment of the day, appears perfunctorily; none of the true nature lover's delight brightens his reports on excursions.

Brown was a romanticist whose ill health cast a melancholy gloom over his thoughts; he meditated on graveyard subjects and on the wisdom of suicide. Interest soon flagged in every activity; he hopped from object to object, task to task. A sense of insufficiency sooner or later lifted him out of every activity, as it had moved him from a stool in a lawyer's office. His parents fondled him and his brothers pitied him. At one moment he strode forth to conquer the world, and at the next he whined in a corner about his cursed fate. When occupied in a congenial task, he worked with unremitting ardor, but when the labor became irksome or when disgust revolted him, he deserted the task with the finality of a child dropping a ball.

In this industrious Quaker family Charles alone was queer. The others entered upon mercantile pursuits, following the family tradition, but Charles became wedded to books and to his peculiar thoughts. He was headstrong, self-willed, conceited, and arrogant. He was "different," a *lusus naturæ* in this soft-spoken, gentle family. It was not that he was ungrateful for their kindness to him, nor that he was unaware of persistent efforts in the council of elders to assist him in finding suitable duties, but he was uncooperative in family and community activities. He liked to exercise his conversational powers in the grand manner of the European salon, and he was happiest when spending his time alone in meditative and scribbling activities.

· 5 ·

Friendship with
Elihu Hubbard Smith

IN SEPTEMBER, 1790, Elihu Hubbard Smith
entered upon a year's study of medicine in Philadelphia. A nineteen-year-old Yale graduate and son of a
physician of Litchfield, Connecticut, Smith had demonstrated precocious talents and unbounded ambition in
science and literature. Despite his youth he saw with
Yankee clarity his opportunities. Under what auspices
we know not, Brown became acquainted with Smith;
their lives became intertwined much as a Virginia creep-
er drapes itself upon a strong oak. Not that Smith was
physically large or robust; his commanding power over
associates emanated from clearly defined aims, relentless pursuit of attainable goals, and willingness to go
into debt to carry out plans. Until the young physician's untimely death in the yellow fever epidemic in
September, 1798, Brown enjoyed almost every kind
of assistance, except complete financial support, which

one youthful contemporary can give another. Each recognized the other's nobility of character; each possessed almost identical liberal views on religion, on man's humanitarian social responsibilities, and on the importance of knowledge as the basic asset in attaining a good personal life. Yet neither wrote many letters to the other, and neither left a record of his impressions of his friend. It is apparent, when we realize that Smith published *Alcuin* at his own expense and doubtless sold the manuscript of *Wieland* to Hocquet Caritat, that Smith was the more forceful, the more energetic in making Brown's dream of a successful literary career come true.

Smith had grown up in the orthodox surroundings of northwest Connecticut. At Yale College, where he was graduated in 1786 at the age of fifteen, he felt the impact of deistic ideas. His orthodox parents sent the lad to the "Puritan Pope," the Reverend Timothy Dwight, then a pastor at Greenfield, Connecticut, for a postgraduate tutorial course in religion. Dwight for a time re-established Smith's faith in Calvinist dogmas, but doubts generated by the study of natural science could not be silenced even by the magisterial assurances of Jonathan Edwards' grandson. As Smith pursued medical studies under Dr. Benjamin Rush and other physicians in what is now the University of Pennsylvania Medical School, he rejected the efficacy of prayer and ceased to pray, he adopted the conclusions of Thomas Paine's *Age of Reason,* and he imbibed the leveling ideas popularized by Rousseau, Condorcet, and Godwin. At moments his sense of departure from tradition aroused terror lest the Connecticut heresy law catch up with him and cause him to return home in disgrace. Yet with intellectual honesty he set forth his heretical opinions in long letters which shocked their conservative recipients; especially concerned was Theodore Dwight, brother of the preacher. Smith became a Godwinian, not so much by reading Godwin as by arriving independently at Godwin's opinions. Smith rejected almost the whole Calvinist theology of God's repressive sovereignty and the doctrines of predestination and total depravity on the ground that God had made a universe in which man might perfect himself through the influence of reason; reason and truth would ultimately prevail through the education of all people, through the consequent dissemination of books, and through the establishment of the ideal of political justice. Although hesitating to adopt Godwin's views on the narrowing of political limits from the nation to the parish, the granting of equality to women, and the theory that all human institutions are oppressive, Smith developed many other liberal opinions and drew the outlines of a Utopia—an imaginary society wherein human perfection might be realized.

Smith either had answers for every question, or he diligently sought them. When a query arose as to the nesting propensities of the bobolink, he wrote to many men for information. When a museum exhibited an elk, he scanned all known publications for information about the strange animal. Restlessly he pursued chemical and botanical knowledge to improve his medical skill; he was a scientist with enthusiastic interest in every aspect of natural lore. Because his work was undertaken before the laboratory had come into existence, the library and not the clinic was the source of his medical knowledge. Conceiving of himself as an aspirant for highest professional honors, he diligently combined the arts of writing and reading with the investigative activity of the scientist; he believed that nothing within human scope was alien to his interests. From his pen flowed verse, an opera, essays, and biographical sketches; he kept a diary, engaged in epistolary interchanges, pursued scientific researches, published one of the first anthologies of American verse, and cofounded the *Medical Repository*, the first magazine devoted solely to scientific research and information in the United States. In the midst of these varied activities he attended regularly a weekly club meeting, visited extensively, joined societies, and served as officer in the Manumission, Hospital, and Geological societies. An almost daily attendant at the theater, he wrote prologues for new plays by his friend William Dunlap. Elihu Hubbard Smith's activities were limited only by his environment.

In his friendship with Brown, Smith evidently attempted to apply some of the principles of Dr. Rush's psychiatry, for the folly of morbid self-pity was quite obvious. By simple means the physician tried to lead Brown to disburden his mind, to examine his true status in life, and then to act resolutely. Yet Brown dwelt fondly upon misfortunes and readily believed himself unfortunate. In a retrospective letter written in 1796, Smith analyzed his friend's status: "You began to fancy that these fictions were real; that you had indeed suffered, enjoyed, known, and seen all that you so long pretended to have experienced; every subsequent event became tinctured with this conviction and accompanied with this diseased apprehension; the habit was formed; and you wandered in a world of your own creation. Now and then a ray of truth broke in upon you, but with an influence too feeble to dissipate the phantoms which errors had conjured up around you. *Godwin came, and all was light.*" Brown gained redirection in life from reading William Godwin's books. A forward-looking philosophy was replacing one of despair; doors were opening toward the sunlight.

When the yellow fever epidemic ravaged Philadelphia in the late summer of 1793, Brown visited Smith, then practicing in Wethersfield, Connecticut. They journeyed to Litchfield, Hartford, and Middletown, Connecticut. At this time Brown made the acquaintance of the Connecticut Wits whose verses Smith had printed in June in *American Poems*. Upon his return to Philadelphia, Brown heard many gruesome tales of the epidemic; this heart-rending episode in the city's life served as a backdrop for two novels, *Ormond* and *Arthur Mervyn*, as well as for incidental pictures in other writings.

In the Philadelphia city directory for 1794 Charles B. Brown is listed as "Master of the Friends' Grammar School" and as residing at "117 N. 2nd Street." The error of North for South has cast some doubt upon the accuracy of the assignment of Brown's occupation. It is quite plausible that, following his rejection of the law, Brown accepted a position as a teacher. After John Todd, the schoolmaster, died in the epidemic, Brown may have taken over the direction of the academy. Yet there is no supporting evidence except that of the directory and the following seemingly autobiographical comment in *Clara Howard:* "The boy was a noble and generous spirit, and endowed with an ardent thirst for knowledge. He . . . became usher in the school in which he had been trained. He was smitten with the charms of literature, and . . . refused to engage in any of those professions which lead to riches and honor. He adopted certain antiquated and unfashionable notions about the 'grandeur of retreat,' 'honorable poverty,' a studious life, and the dignity of imparting knowledge to others."

Among Smith's friends was William Johnson, a lawyer and a Yale graduate of the class of 1788, who, absent from Connecticut during Brown's visit, promised to look in on Brown during a journey to Philadelphia. Johnson failed to appear. In a letter of February 13, 1794, Brown expressed disappointment at not meeting Johnson and proposed a correspondence: "My pen will never be quite as communicative as my tongue. I should, however, if circumstances permitted, be inclined to send you a much more loquacious letter than this will prove, the purpose of which, indeed, is rather to provoke an answer than to indulge a talkative propensity, and to procure the pleasure of one or two lines from you. Were I not fearful of the imputation of vanity, I might urge claims to your confidence and friendship yielding only to fraternal ties." Here is eloquent testimony of Brown's attitude toward Smith, whom he held in such high esteem that a friend of Smith seemed almost as close as a brother. These sentences also suggest something of Brown's eager enlistment of new friends among young men of his own age; he sought orientation this way. Soon Johnson and Brown would grasp hands in New York City under Smith's roof and cement their friendship through daily meetings.

On September 5, 1793, after two years in Wethersfield, Connecticut, Smith opened an office for the practice of medicine in New York. Now twenty-three and alone, for he did not apprentice himself to an older physician, he awaited calls that seldom came. With letters of introduction from Dr. Lemuel Hopkins and Dr. Mason F. Cogswell, Smith sought out Yale men and physicians to announce his presence. At the office of the first daily newspaper, the New York *Minerva*, he greeted Noah Webster, fresh from a law office in Hartford and already the most forceful editor in the metropolis, daily engaged in combating political and medical error. Webster took a liking to the young physician and confirmed this confidence by summoning him to vaccinate, and to diagnose the ailments of, the Webster children. Webster was rising to be one of the most influential men in New York City Federalist political circles. Still in his mind was a plan to compile a great American dictionary which would drive Dr. Samuel Johnson's book from the shelves of learned men in the United States, but the drudgery of the newspaper office prevented much activity in this self-imposed nationalistic task. In an effort to secure the necessary relief, Webster proposed that Smith drop medicine and become managing editor of the *Minerva*. Although Smith refused, Webster continued to cherish affection for the physician.

As a Yale man, Smith quickly entered cordial relations with other alumni of the New Haven college. William W. and Gurdon M. Woolsey introduced Smith to William Dunlap, the painter, dramatist, and theater manager, who was their brother-in-law. William Johnson took rooms with Smith at 45 Pine Street. Lynde Catlin, Prosper Wetmore, Thomas Mumford, and Horace and Seth Johnson, brothers of William, also were in the city. This group formed the original ten members of the Friendly Club, a society designed to assist the members in keeping abreast of current intellectual progress through weekly meetings on Saturday nights at the homes of the members. The program consisted usually of the reading by the chairman of selections from a periodical or book. Then the group ruminated upon this morsel until its flavor was gone; thereafter they fell into conversation about trade, politics, literature, and their family affairs. When Catlin married and showed greater fondness for his wife than for the Club, he was replaced by James Kent, the young barrister who was soon to teach law at Columbia College and then rise to the chancellorship of the Supreme Court of New York State. In his ascent he would remember to take William Johnson with him as Clerk of Court and to dedicate to this friend of his college and early professional days the monumental *Commentaries on American Law* (1826-1830). With the removal of Mumford from New York, Charles Adams, son of President John Adams, was admitted to membership, but he withdrew soon after his marriage. Attendance averaged five or six members, although at one meeting in 1796 ten members duly appeared at Kent's. Visitors occasionally joined them. Richard Alsop, the poet and merchant, attended several times, as did Henry Gahn, a Swedish immigrant. After Smith had been drawn into professional union with Dr. Edward Miller in the foundation of the *Medical Repository,* this gentleman joined the group. Dunlap asserts that the membership included the Reverend Samuel Miller, author of *A Brief Retrospect of the Eighteenth Century;* Dr. Samuel Latham Mitchill, the scientist and statesman; Anthony Bleeker, John Wells, and Charles Brockden Brown. In the extant volumes of Smith's diaries there is no evidence that these men were admitted formally to membership before May, 1798, although Brown attended meetings fairly regularly during his long visits to New York City.

This club was not interested in provoking original compositions nor was it an organization fostering a national literature; rather it was a group of young men in their early twenties anxious to have congenial companions with whom to discuss the ideas of Hume, Priestley, Godwin, Condorcet, and other political thinkers. On occasion topics drawn from natural science were introduced, but by far the greatest attention was given to political subjects.

Through Adams the members met John Adams, then Vice-President of the United States. The group invited Dr. Timothy Dwight, president of Yale from 1795 to 1817, and other distinguished men to sit with them, but seldom was the group favored with the presence of older men. James Watson, the merchant and politician, and Samuel Miles Hopkins attended several times. By and large, the Friendly Club gave Brown and Dunlap little more encouragement in their creative activity than would be given today by a New York alumni chapter of a college fraternity; there would be expressions of interest and possibly a program devoted to the reading of excerpts. Beyond this no help could be given, for the writing of plays and novels is a lonely business, carried on in solitude at home and not in the midst of a circle of admiring but uncritical friends interested in politics.

First Attempt at Fiction

IN THE summer of 1794 Brown visited Smith in New York. Now began an intimacy with William Dunlap and the members of the Friendly Club. In Dunlap the tremulous Quaker found an inspiring model, for the dramatist had produced his first comedy of manners at twenty-three, the age of Brown at the time of their meeting. Other writings, in prose, verse, and drama, were turned out by Dunlap with an ease comparable to Brown's own facility. But where Dunlap began and finished one work at a time, Brown began eagerly with an idea, pursued it briefly, lost interest, and dropped the topic as uninteresting. However much he yearned for a literary career, Brown lacked the necessary control. Yet something occurred on this visit to cause him to dedicate himself anew to authorship. In August, Brown wrote to Dunlap: "My excursion to New York will be remembered by me with the most pleasing emotions."

First Attempt at Fiction

Evidently Smith's plans for a second volume of *American Poems* aroused the three friends to compete for space therein. Brown's only known verse of the year, dated September, 1794, was printed in the *American Register* for 1808. "Devotion—an Epistle," a misty blank verse autobiography, gives insight into Brown's thoughts in the years immediately following his surrender of law. A restless dream-wanderer in the realm of learning, he conjured up bright visions of ethereal maidens whose sole duty would be to rescue him from the sable troop of infernal spirits haunting his mind. Like Poe's many years later, Brown's thoughts gravitated naturally to morbid topics now generally classed in the realm of abnormal psychology. It is not surprising, therefore, that his best writing should have been done in terror fiction in which effectiveness depended upon the generation of emotions similar to those which nearly drove him to the brink of suicide.

In a letter to Wilkins, Brown expressed his utter unworthiness to play a useful part in life:

I have not been deficient in the pursuit of that necessary branch of knowledge, the study of myself. . . . I long ago discovered that nature had not qualified me for an actor on this stage. The nature of my education only added to these disqualifications, and I experienced all those deviations from the center which arise when all our lessons are taken from books. . . . No man ought to act but in pursuance to some rational motive, and what useful purpose could be answered by making C. B. B. better known to his friends? What but their unhappiness could be produced by it? Forget me, my friend, as soon as possible. . . . I am neither incorrigibly stupid nor remorselessly wicked. I am a lover and admirer of all that is good and fair in the moral universe. No one gazes at genius with more enthusiastic delight and admiration, or at virtue with greater love and reverence. . . . I seize anything, however weak and dubious, by which I can hope to raise myself from that profound abyss of ignominy and debasement into which I am sunk by my own reflections.

These sentences reveal something of Brown's tendency to write letters of great length in a misty, hinting manner, suggesting all manner of ills and yet describing none. Prey to melancholy, his mind rambled amid the dark shapes of a nether world, neither comprehending their meaning nor allowing them to interfere with his daily life. Brown's eldest brother, aware of this tendency, wrote over a period of eight years numerous admonitory letters, the gist of which was the wisdom "of covering from the eyes of others with an impenetrable mask whatever fears or anxieties may agitate us." Smith, Dunlap, and Johnson later became annoyed at this secretive sinuosity, for they spent much effort in trying to keep the doubter afloat when he appeared to be sinking.

An instance of strange behavior occurred in Philadelphia, on October 29, 1794, when Dunlap produced his new tragedy, *The Fatal Deception; or, The Progress of Guilt*, later named *Leicester*. Brown accompanied the dramatist to the theater, but hesitated to express an opinion of either the play or the performers. After the lapse of a month, on November 28, 1794, Brown wrote that he did not think theatrical people entitled to encomiums, that his imagination was too undisciplined by experience to distinguish the dramatic from the merely theatrical elements in a performance, and that he had abandoned all desire to be a dramatist: "My sufferings during that evening were such as to make me unalterably determined never to be an author. That, indeed, was not before scarcely possible, but if every other circumstance were favorable, the dread of being torn and mangled by the playhouse gentry, either of the stage or pit, would sufficiently damp my ardor." The tragedy was indeed bad. Its wretched verse and melodramatic action were almost as unpardonable as the license taken with historical fact. Any friend of the author must have writhed as the shoddy performance proceeded. Yet in spite of unwillingness to pen "undistinguishing encomiums," Brown hinted that the play was generally satisfactory. Such was the hesitancy with which the members of the Friendly Club spoke of each other's writings; surely there was little aliment for genius in this tongue-tied sensibility.

No poet in the 1790's could well escape the pressure to be "wholly American" in subject matter and point of view. In his own verse Brown had done little to reflect popular opinion. Yet he wrote to Dunlap thus:

It used to be a favorite maxim with me that the genius of a poet should be sacred to the glory of his country. How far this rule can be reduced to practice by an American bard, how far he can prudently observe it, and what success has crowned the efforts of those who in their compositions have shown that they have not been unmindful of it, is perhaps worth the inquiry. National songs, strains which have a peculiar relation to the political or religious transactions of the poet's country, seem to be the most precious morsels which do not require a dissatisfying brevity nor preclude the most exalted flights of genius, for in this class I rank the *Iliad* and *Aeneid* and *Orlando* (the last is a truly national song, since the streets of every Italian city have re-echoed with it for this hundred years or two), as well as "Chevy Chase" or the "Song of Roland."

Does it not appear to you that to give poetry a popular currency and universal reputation, a particular cast of manners and state of civilization is necessary? I have sometimes thought so, but perhaps it is an error, and the want of popular poems argues only the demerit of those who have already written or some defect in their works which unfits them for every taste or understanding.

The pen of the Philadelphian doubtless scratched endlessly during the winter of 1794-1795. Not a bit of biographical information survives for this period. In the summer of 1795 Brown again visited his friends. Dunlap generally spent his summers in Perth Amboy, New Jersey, and here Brown went for an extended visit. In September, after returning to Philadelphia, Brown wrote exultantly of progress on his "Philadelphia novel," probably *Arthur Mervyn:* "Soon after my return I began the design of which we talked so much. I had planned so that I could finish a work equal in extent to *Caleb Williams* in less than six weeks; and I wrote a quantity equivalent to ten of [Godwin's] pages daily, till the hot weather and inconvenient circumstances obliged me to relax my diligence. Great expedition does not seem very desirable. Tenets so momentous require a leisurely and deep examination; and much meditation, reading, and writing, I presume, are necessary to render my system of morality perfect in all its parts, and to acquire a full and luminous conviction; but I have not stopped—I go on, though less precipitately than at first—and I hope finally to produce something valuable for its utility."

On October 17, 1795, Smith made the following notation in his diary: "I can account for my not having heard from C. B. Brown only by supposing him busily engaged in his Work. . . . I feel no small curiosity to see how my friend will manage his plot. But I have no doubt of its being worthy of its author. What different sentiments it will excite! and how much rancor and misrepresentation must he encounter! And not he alone, but all those who are united to him by the ties of friendship and the bonds of resembling opinions. Hitherto, in respect to public performances, our lives have glided forward smoothly enough. A calm like this can not be durable. Storms and tempests hover over our heads ready to burst or are gathering in slow and sullen vengeance to break and overwhelm us with destruction. But I trust that we shall put forth the conductors of virtue, and turn aside or disarm the lightnings of superstitious fury." Apparently the new novel was to set forth the liberal, rationalistic, Godwinian philosophy which these young men had adopted in preference to the traditional beliefs of their own sects.

On January 1, 1796, Smith appeared in Philadelphia as a delegate to the Manumission Society convention. At once he called on Brown; during the next ten days the friends spent many hours reading or hearing por-

tions of the new novel. "After wandering through
fifty pages," Brown realized that he was "unfitted
for the instructor's chair" as a moralist, and that his
feeble and diffuse style fell short of his lofty aim.
The plan of this lost work fits in closely with that of
Arthur Mervyn, and doubtless some of these pages in
strengthened form, rather than speed in composition,
account for the publication of the first nine chapters
of *Arthur Mervyn* in 1798 at the time *Wieland* was
being printed.

Dunlap had written friendly letters to Godwin and
Holcroft, much as if the three American writers stood
ready to join an international alliance of liberal writers.
The replies were "of such a sort as might be expected
from the authors of those works which we read together
with so much delight," wrote Smith, who added: "Let
these communications strengthen your heart and give
new activity to your hands. We must do something to
convince these men that we are worthy to receive some
moments of their consideration." Smith again was
applying the goad to the laggard's ambition.

But Brown in the course of the following spring
evidently fell into another melancholy mood; on May
7, 1796, Smith played psychiatrist in a long letter
which deserves extensive quotation:

Your letter, my dear Charles, was the occasion of
much satisfaction, as well as disappointment and sorrow,
to your friends. Sentiments so opposite, yet so intimately combined and interwoven, gave it an interest
in our hearts which sensibility could not but cherish,
and which reason hesitated whether she should welcome
or disclaim. Why is it so? Wherefore are you so

vigorous, so firm in thought; and so weak, so vacillating in action? Charles! Charles! if thou hast not strength to contend with the tempter,—if thou art not mighty enough to overcome temptation and trample it under thy foot,—doth not wisdom whisper thee to decline the combat and to fly the field? To encounter danger, to brave death causelessly and with the certainty of suffering,—the mildest appellation for such conduct is folly; and the person who is guilty of it can only be excused on the plea of disordered intellect. By heaven! my friend! I mourn and am afflicted for you—for myself—(for to my own weakness, does this reproof reach) and I "could play the woman with my eyes," if haply it might warn you to retire or animate you to conquer.

We must know our errors, or how can we correct them? We must be informed of their whole extent, of their utmost virulence, or how can we apply the remedy? He deserves not the name of physician, who, thro' fear of giving pain, temporizes with his patient, when the ulcer threatens his life and requires instant extirpation. To wound is to save; to delay is to destroy. No palliative can reach this case. Nay, tho' it seems to menace but little danger, tho' returning sanity appear to glow around its edges, trust not! withhold not! the poison sinks inward; a moment, and it preys upon the vitals.

You "have been the child of passion and inconsistency, the slave of desires that can not be honorably gratified, the slave of hopes no less criminal than fantastic." What, my friend, is the meaning of all this? And what am I to learn from it? Or, rather, what are *we*—Dunlap and Smith—to learn from it? If you meant that we should understand you, why were you not explicit? If you had no such intention, where was the necessity of introducing such a passage? Charles! you know we love you. Your heart has told you so a thousand times; and you *dare not* question it! You know too that *real friends* alone have the courage to point out the faults of others boldly to themselves. You know the difficulty, the delicacy, the danger of the undertaking. You are well aware of the value of sincerity; you see that we stand, as it were, isolated from the rest of mankind; and you must be convinced that if we are not true to ourselves and true to each other, we can not hope for aid, correction, and instruction—candidly and affectionately administered—from any one besides: for the world troubles not itself with these things, or minds them only to the injury of the individual.

This is a solemn strain, you will say, a melancholy and grave preface. It is—and indeed, my Charles, the occasion requires it. Why do you so much delight in mystery? Is it the disease of will? or of habit? Do you, of choice, give to the simplest circumstances the air of fiction or have you been so long accustomed to deal in visionary scenes, to intertwine the real with the imaginary, and to enwrap yourself in the mantle of ambiguous seeming, that your pen involuntarily borrows the phraseology of fancy, and by the spell of magic words still diffuses round you the mist of obscuring uncertainty? The man of Truth, Charles! the pupil of Reason has no mysteries. He knows that former errors do not constitute him guilty now; he has nothing to conceal. He seeks only to know his duty and perform it, and he has no occasion for disguise. He places with his own hand the window in his breast; and he bids the world look in and comment. Lurks there any deformity within, he blesses the eye that descries it, commends the tongue that proclaims, and kisses the hand that drags it to the light. He acknowledges his error; he owns his weakness; he purifies his heart; and he invigorates his hands.

What do your most intimate friends, my Charles,

[*58*]

know of you? What do they wish to know, but that they may be of use to you? Far be from them that teasing curiosity which seeks only its own gratification. If there be any thing you think it your duty to withhold from them, withhold it; they will not blame you. If there be any thing you have not the courage to reveal, conceal it still. They will not commend the cowardice, but they will compassionate, will pardon it. But when you know that these are their feelings, why still do you continue to remind them that there are secrets? that you have science [knowledge] which they must not have? Why will you allude to misfortunes of which they are ignorant, and from which, therefore, they can not relieve you? Why will you array each new transaction in the garb of obscurity? Are you, yourself, conscious how much this is a prevailing fault, both in your speech and writing? In this very letter to which I am replying in a sort, we only learn by implication that Joseph [Bringhurst] has been imprisoned. The fact is nowhere plainly noted; had it not been for his letter, I had still remained somewhat doubtful whether you meant he had been in prison or not. It would have been much more agreeable to us both—D. and S.— to have been informed simply of the fact; and the circumstances of it. Again, when you mention the authors you have read—instead of a plain account of them—we behold you with visionary step printing the sands of Arabia, hovering over the hills of Switzerland on wings of imagination, and exploring the wilds of America with the eye of fiction. I particularize because you have sometimes complained of our want of precision when we have attempted to point out your errors. I confess that the style of these remarks of yours is handsome; in a poem I should have been charmed with it, but in a letter a mere catalogue, with a slight notice of the character of each book, would have given me much better information. And in such

cases it is information we look for—not amusement—
and the more simply and precisely it is conveyed, the
better. Besides we are apt to distrust information so
conveyed; and we ought to distrust it, for it often
imposes on and misleads us. The pen of poesy, Charles,
is not often that of philosophy and truth. But I will
have done with this language—only commending the
word *simplicity* to be inserted in capitals in your vocabulary.

Stung to the quick, Brown replied at once, on May
10, in a letter which has been lost. Smith's first draft
of a reply written on May 27 repeated the charges
leveled against the novelist:

. . . You are not charged with intentional misrepresentation of the truth, but with conveying it in such a
manner as to make it difficult of comprehension to
your friends, or encumbered with such circumstances
or deficient in such particularities as to render it unintelligible to them. Here is no charge of falsifying
the truth. Here are no doubts expressed of your veracity. Here is no more than a plain intimation of an
erroneous manner of communicating information, which
those who love you regard as a misfortune—as an
error—persisted in by you, through ignorance, and
capable of being remedied by you when fairly exposed
to your contemplation.
Among the number of our conversations at Amboy,
some, you will recollect, turned on the subject of
your style of composition. It was charged with certain defects by us, and we endeavored to make you
sensible to them. We were unsuccessful. In the epistolary communications which succeeded, we could not
but discern the same faults. The sense was often
obscured by imperfect metaphors, tumultuously heaped

upon each other; common facts were introduced with a species of poetical periphrasis which sometimes puzzled us to determine what was and what was not accurate; and allusions were made to transactions in relation to which we could neither act nor speak, neither aid nor counsel you—as all on our part was conjecture and obscurity. It became necessary for us to renew our remonstrances on this point; and your letter, in answer to which my last was written, as it offered several examples of the defects we complain of, was made the subject or basis of our friendly reprehensions. The manner in which you communicated to us the names of the authors and the titles of their works which you had been reading was faulty, as it wanted both perspicuity and precision. The passage in regard to Bringhurst, as I have before remarked, was so obscure as to leave me in doubt. You talked of the terror he had conceived of imprisonment, the value he set upon unimpeached integrity, &c., from which I concluded that he had been in jail and had been declared insolvent, &c., but the plain facts would have been more acceptable. Knowing his character, it would not be difficult to make the proper inferences. Now in respect to both these instances of a faulty mode of communicating on your part, you will not find that we have charged you with intentional "mystery and delusion." An instance occurs in your letter before me of a similar fault when, speaking of Mr. Laffert, you say, "He resides in the rural neighborhood of this city." I know where he lives, but what information would a stranger derive from that passage? You see, I do not question your veracity: I take it for granted that Mr. Lt. does "reside in the rural neighborhood" of Phila., but what am I the wiser? Unless it be that I learn that he does not reside in the city?

How have you been "the slave of passion and inconsistency"? And what are these "desires which can not be honorably gratified? that are no less criminal than fantastic"? Do you not see that this partial communication is nugatory? That we can address to you neither counsel nor instruction—in short, can not be of the least possible service to you in these respects without precise information? If you wished our assistance, it was your duty to point out explicitly wherein we could assist you, to have discovered to us the nature of your danger and the causes of your weakness. If you either did not need our aid or resolved neither to request nor accept it, why make such a communication? To what purpose could it subserve? Surely none, since we could not "usefully animadvert" upon it; and you were determined not "to be benefited by the disclosure."

Here, then, is the point between us, here is the matter of which I complain, that you will allude to circumstances which you do not choose to explain, and which, therefore, are foreign to the purpose of our correspondence, since without explanation we can render you no assistance in regard to them. Not that I question your veracity when you assure me that you have been unfortunate, but that I am pained to be the useless depository of complaints I can not understand, of sorrows that I can not assuage.

I do not mean to call upon you for explanations. I do not want to know to what you allude. I can not find fault with your conduct in concealing the circumstances of your early fortunes, since I neither know what you conceal nor the motives you have for concealment. I am actuated but by one wish in relation to you—to be of service to you and to render you useful to mankind. To effect this wish, I am willing to receive what you choose to communicate if, by my animadversions or opinions on such communications, I can advance your welfare. But I do not love to be needlessly perplexed and grieved; neither should you needlessly add to my perplexity and sorrow.

In respect to your former communications, relative to the story of yourself,—tho' I meant not in my last letter to allude to them,—I acknowledge in all sincerity and simplicity of heart I know not what to believe. You have acknowledged that you *once* thought yourself at liberty to vary circumstances in the narration, and in those fragments which have been related to me I find so many and such perfect contradictions that I am forced to suspend my belief on all, as I can reconcile but few of them to each other. This has formerly been the cause of much pain to me on your account; it is so no longer. I suppose that hereafter, should it seem proper in you to disclose the facts, the disclosure will be accurate. In the meantime I have no curiosity; and my only wish is that you, by avoiding all allusions to these events of your life, would neither excite doubt nor alarm sensibility.

This letter is long, and I am weary with writing; you will excuse me, therefore, for passing over, for the present at least, some parts of your letter. But I can not forbear to add, on the subject which is now before us, that it does appear to me that, at some former periods of your life, you affected to be mysterious and made ambiguity your delight. That the example of J. J. Rousseau had too many charms in your eyes not to captivate you and incite you to imitate him, and that you were pleased to have others believe those misfortunes to be real which you knew how so eloquently to describe. The transition is natural, to a mind of sensibility almost unavoidable. You began to fancy that these fictions were real; that you had indeed suffered, enjoyed, known, and seen all that you had so long pretended to have experienced; every subsequent event became tinctured with this conviction and accompanied with this diseased apprehension; the habit was formed; and you wandered in a world of your own creation. Now and then a ray of truth broke in upon you, but with an influence too feeble to dissipate the phantoms which error had conjured up around you. *Godwin came, & all was light.* —But the Sun himself does not always diffuse around us his benignant beams; clouds and mists sometimes intervene and shut him from our view. Despair itself is dear to the wretch who has drunk deep of the delicious potion of Love. Cold, cruel tho' she be, dead to honor and "glorying in her shame," the form he loves is dear to him: he fosters, he cherishes her idea in his heart; it is his ruin, but he can not resolve to loose it. With what gradual, what scarce perceptible advance to reason, to activity, to virtue! How often does he relapse into his woe, call upon the phantom of his passion, and banquet on the pleasures of despair! Nay, when full of mighty purposes of reformation, how often does his self-love cheat him of his resolution, his actions burst out in all the extravagance, his voice swell with all the emphasis of passion—while he smiles upon the cheat!

See you any points of resemblance in this picture, Charles, and a friend of ours that shall be nameless?

In the absence of further letters and specific evidence, it is not possible to indicate whether the budding novelist seriously reviewed his habits or attempted to correct his errors. The old faults continued almost unchanged. The physician had diagnosed the patient's ailment correctly, but the prescription was apparently unpalatable.

Late in July, 1796, Brown joined Dunlap in Perth

Amboy, where the latter with his wife and son had gone to escape the heat of New York City. Here in the presence of the one eminent literary man he was to know intimately, Brown expanded and flourished like a seed brought to fruition in a fertile soil. Smith appeared for a five-day visit on August 4; as he embraced Brown, he remarked: "I have never seen you look so well." Brown replied that he had been unwell for months. They then fell into lively conversation on their favorite themes of man, morals, and politics. Gently Smith asked Brown about the novel, only to learn that the manuscript had been tossed into a corner. A few pages of diary jottings alone testified to Brown's literary interest.

Smith then explained his plans for a drama based upon the seventh volume of Helen Maria Williams' *Letters,* in which an idealistic young man with lofty thoughts of humanity frees prisoners arrested during the French Revolution. Dunlap and Brown, seeing merit in the plot, approved the design and suggested subordinate incidents. The flame of the Philadelphian's ambition again flared. He wondered whether New York City might not lift him from lethargy into endeavor, whether the presence of these two friends might not cure the cursed megrim pains resulting from indecision, and whether the time had not come for engaging in serious literary tasks. Smith phrased the galvanizing effect of the friends' conversations and thus clarified the motives of Brown: "Their conversation is too valuable, their united aid in the sublime occupation too rare to make me hesitate for a single moment in preferring my present occupation. . . .

From conferences such as these, new intellectual as well as moral energy is derived; a fresh spring is given every noble exertion, and a bolder, firm point of support is formed for all future benevolent undertakings. *'It is good for us to be here.'* "

On August 7 the three friends went for a walk to revisit a tripartite tree, emblem of their friendship, which they had discovered and made their own a year earlier. There was no doubt which part belonged to each, for each had fixed upon his own. They readily agreed that the slenderest one, which grew in the middle, was Brown's. The stouter boles symbolized the stronger men who sustained their weaker friend. There is no more touching incident in the record of early national American literature than this of two young authors befriending a third to assure the production of those great writings which trembled on the verge of birth, but which would never be born until conditions became favorable.

Brown remained in Perth Amboy through August. Here with the dramatist, whose circle of friends embraced the whole community, Brown recovered from despair and formulated literary plans sufficient to occupy him for years. Above all else came the decision to cast loose from his Philadelphia home and to establish himself in New York City. Like Smith and Johnson, he moved to the city with ample funds supplied by his family. Although each husbanded his resources with some care, none found it necessary to relinquish season tickets at the theater or skimp expenditures for clothing and meals. Each would, now and again, lament the high cost of living and write regretful letters on the painful subject of borrowing from father, but each maintained the ménage proper to young bachelors with well-to-do parents.

Brown's Feet Touch Earth

WHEN Brown crossed the Hudson River to New York City on September 1, 1796, he cast his lot with a city that was rapidly outdistancing his native Philadelphia in size and commercial importance. The population was little more than 25,000, and the city proper reached no farther north than what is now Washington Square; yet nature had favored the city with a location destined to give it a commanding commercial position. Where international trade is readily carried on, there a metropolis inevitably will develop. Young men from the back country, such as those constituting the Friendly Club, moved to New York and established themselves in business, law, or medicine, or risked careers in literature and the fine arts. Lynde Catlin, a Yale graduate of 1786, began as a teller in the United States Bank, and soon was president of the Merchants Bank. John Wells, whose family had been murdered by Indians in Otsego County, New

York, came to the law by way of Princeton. Prosper
Wetmore, who soldiered in the Revolutionary War
in 1781 at the age of fourteen, engaged in the China
and West India trade. William and Gurdon Woolsey
were merchants, and William Dunlap, when the theater languished, opened a draper's shop and measured
calico and silk for fashionable ladies. But Brown,
who had seen enough of law offices and mercantile establishments in Philadelphia, turned his back
on worldly pursuits. The muse, not money, was his
master. While his companions went into the market-
place daily to sell their wares to the highest bidder,
he remained in his rooms with his books and quill pens
and fresh white paper.

An orgy of European speculation energized the
financial world late in 1796. Lawyers were everywhere in demand to draw agreements, to interpret
the "fine print," and to act as conveyancers. American politics felt the repercussions of events abroad.
When President Washington refused to stand for re-
election for a third term, John Adams and Thomas
Jefferson became the active candidates. The American two-party system grew out of this rivalry. The
Federalists had brought Noah Webster to New York
City to publicize their doctrines and support their
candidates in a daily newspaper. As the tempo of
political argument stepped up, as party hostilities
flared into open combat, Webster withdrew to a scholar's study. Charles Adams, eldest and beloved son
of the presidential candidate, gave his young associates unimpeachably authoritative information. Webster similarly passed along political gossip, although

his "immaculate paper" never descended to mudslinging antics. Brown watched the trend of events more with a moralist's concern to discover theoretical remedies which might be described in romances than to participate in the hurly-burly of political quarreling.

Brown's life in New York involved, usually, breakfast with Smith and Johnson, a period of writing or reading each morning and afternoon, an hour or two of conversation with Smith each day, and calls on friends or attendance at the theater in the evening. The physician, who followed a carefully planned routine whereby he might keep abreast of his many interests, jotted in his diary the effect of the novelist's presence: "The circumstance which at present appears most likely to impede my progress in my destined course is the presence of my friend, C. B. Brown. His society is too pleasing, his conversation too interesting, and his pursuits too important and connected with my own, not to engage an unusual share of my attention and my time. In his company, in that of my other friends as united with him and occupied in the discussion of so many high and extensive principles of policy and morals, it is not impossible that I may oftentimes forget to 'build the lofty rhyme,' to 'exhibit the exact impress and body' of my friends [in biographical essays], to trace the mysterious windings of disease, and to lay the aerial foundations of the visionary republic of Utopia."

Among Brown's pursuits was the composition of "a new political romance," the first portion of which he read to Smith on October 17, 1796. This work doubtless is *Sketches of a History of Carsol*. But

ten days later Brown appeared with "some notes toward his *great plan,* drawn from reading Coxe's *Russian Discoveries*"; no further information concerning
this work survives.

Carsol is a novel with a pseudo-historical basis. It
concerns the island Carsol and its ruler, King Arthur,
who between 1650 and 1680 attempts to return the
kingdom to its ancient independence as established by
his ancestor, Charles Martel, in 1300. Arthur wishes
to free Carsol from the domination of the Roman
Catholic Church, partly because its immense reve-
nues are not contributed to "the real instruction of
the people," and partly because Catholicism has replaced an ancient national religion. To hasten reform,
Arthur has caused a book, *Carsola Restaurata,* to be
written to dramatize the contrast between the present decay of the Church with the purity existing in
Martel's day, and "to bring back the theory of the
Carsol government to that pattern."

As printed in Dunlap's *Life,* the jumbled fragments of this tale describe the revolutionary activity
of Piero Hecta in 1550, the fifty-seven-year reign of
terror of Michael Praya who followed Hecta, the
continuous warfare between the Carsolians and the
Mohammedans between 1300 and 1550, and, finally,
the reign of Alexandra IV (1597-1631) and the four
succeeding Alexanders who fostered a native religion.

The confused order of materials in *Carsol* is the
result either of an editor's careless shuffling of the
manuscript or of the author's writing of isolated sections which later were to be joined with connecting
links. The appearance in the text of the date 1805

indicates that the work was taken up at intervals with some hope of bringing order to its chaos. Here appears an almost complete ineptitude for historical narrative: there is no description, no conversation; all is summary, all is general. The characters are not particularized. The pattern of historical fiction, except as found in epic poems and possibly in a few Gothic novels, was not known. The fumbling toward form apparently led to an imitation of Gibbon's orotund *Decline and Fall of the Roman Empire,* but at no point could the young American clothe invented facts with imaginative fullness or surround them with a body of interpretative comment paralleling the historian's. Hasty, dull generalization striding through the centuries cannot serve as a substitute for the dramatic clash of personalities in moments of crisis.

Doubtless begun at the same time and added to in 1805 was *Sketches of the History of the Carrils and Ormes,* a more chaotic marshaling of materials than *Carsol.* The history of religious nationalism in England is traced from the establishment of Christianity by Arthur in A.D. 70. With a chain given by St. Paul as testimony of his apostolic authority, he establishes a shrine at Cær Arthur or Carthew. The transmission of this religion through the fifteenth century is described to extol the saintly life of Pamphela. The narrative then recounts the rise of the Carril family and its union with the Ormes, a complicated genealogical affair.

Walter Carril is singled out for special attention because of his drunkenness, promiscuity, immorality, and cruelty. His wife, Louisa Boyle, and his twin daughters, Mary and Elizabeth, flee to Philadelphia in 1774. When Walter dies as a sot, his mother keeps the son's embalmed body in her room. Here Brown has material of the type found in *Arthur Mervyn* and *Edgar Huntly*. In contrast with Walter, Arthur and Herbert Orme grow up to be stalwart young men, anxious to maintain the family position. Herbert travels in America, meets Elizabeth Carril, and woos her successfully. Mary marries Mr. Sale, who dies soon and leaves open the way for her marriage to Coulthurst. Announcement of a legacy in England leads to a secret marriage. She goes to England in 1800, and there Arthur Carril asks her to keep secret her connection with Coulthurst. Not until December, 1804, is Coulthurst permitted to join his wife, and then only after being shipwrecked. This passage has the later Brown quality; it doubtless was inserted in 1805 as a means of lending interest to an otherwise dull exposition.

Paul Allen, the original compiler of Dunlap's biography of Brown, explained the fragments thus: "Those sketches must all be considered as introductory to his favorite prospect of a perfect system of government." This statement has in its support almost no evidence in the text, but since the substance concerns political matters there may be some plausibility in the explanation.

Whatever the reason, the romancer was not faithful in attendance at the meetings of the Friendly Club in the autumn of 1796. He listened to M. Roulet, a Swiss immigrant whom he tutored in English, discourse on the implications of the French Revolution to America. He skipped the meeting of October 8 when Smith read two ballads of Bürger, and again was absent two weeks later. On the 29th William Johnson read from Thucydides. The evening's discussion is thus reported in Smith's diary: "Fell at last on the old subject of Truth. Many difficulties. Woolsey, Johnson, and I maintain that *on all occasions* truth is to be spoken: that is, that nothing will justify a falsehood; or that utility can never be promoted thereby. Brown and Dunlap pretend that tho' our position is *generally* true, yet there are occasions when it will be our duty to speak falsely, since by so doing we shall promote the general good. Long discussion—grounds of argument gone over several times—no conclusions."

Brown remained uninterruptedly in New York City until March 16, 1797. During the autumn and winter his routine remained the same, except that more and more time was spent each day in Smith's rooms. Now resident physician in the hospital, Smith gained much experience with immigrants and other charity patients. With co-editors Dr. Edward Miller and Dr. Samuel Latham Mitchill, he had moved forward steadily in developing plans for the publication of the *Medical Repository*. For this magazine Smith wrote the prospectus, several essays, and dozens of letters to physicians throughout the nation. Yet these professional activities permitted time for tinkering at verse, refurbishing for production on December 19, 1796, his opera, *Edwin and Angelina*, and beginning the dramatization of popular English novels and the translation of French deistic tracts.

Dunlap likewise was busily engaged in writing new

plays. On October 31, 1796, his tragedy, *The Mysterious Monk,* was produced for the first time, and on November 12 a new comedy, *Tell Truth and Shame the Devil,* was read to the Friendly Club. Smith opined: "I fear it is too moral to succeed. Our audiences must have a plentiful dose of fun to make even a drop of morality palatable." In January, 1797, Dunlap read scenes from *The Fall of Robespierre.* In this month, too, nineteen-year-old John Blair Linn brought his drama, *Bourville Castle,* to Brown and Dunlap for correction.

The challenge of accomplishment was flung daily by these men. Each used his pen in behalf of American cultural advancement and thus provided an enviable example. But the friends worked directly, too. One might hear Smith or Dunlap say, "Now, Charles, why don't you write about——?" It was in response to such encouragement that Brown began a dramatization of Robert Bage's novel *Hermsprong.* In the twentieth volume of the *Monthly Review,* Smith found a reference to Hoozuana, a race of men with utopian physical qualities of great strength, agility, temperance, acute vision, and insensibility to changes of temperature. "Here," wrote Smith in his diary, on November 20, 1796, "is a notion for the purposes of Ch. B. Brown." Six days later Smith procured the third volume of Benjamin Gooch's *Chirurgical Works* "for the purpose of showing Brown the 'History of the Sleepless Man of Madrid,' a history which is connected with many important speculations." Brown's interest in medical anomalies and abnormal psychology, as evidenced in his four major novels, obviously was fostered by this association. Yet these suggestions seldom were adopted, for the young novelist had romantic ideas of his own. On December 14 Smith remarked: "I wish he would turn his Aloas and Astoias, his Buttiscoes and Carlovingas to some account. He starts an idea, pursues it a little way; new ones spring up; he runs a short distance after each; meantime the original one is likely to escape entirely." What these writings were we cannot now learn, but it appears that Brown was dabbling in the same sort of moralized pseudo-historical romance as *Carsol*.

Wide reading as well as ineffectual scribbling marked this six-month stay in New York City. The new English novels, *Hermsprong, Camilla*, and a dozen others, passed around the circle of friends. The British magazines, especially the London *Monthly Review*, were discussed eagerly in the Club. Here first was mentioned the name of Christoph Martin Wieland, then acclaimed Germany's leading poet, a family name Brown later adopted for the hero in his first published novel. In the *New Annual Register* were described the singularities of John Howard, the philanthropist, who as high sheriff of Bedford, England, had investigated the penal system and had exposed its many horrifying abuses. Here was a prototype of Arthur Mervyn. Count Rumford's *Essays* provided the astonishing fact, included in *Ormond*, that in time of plague one can subsist for three months wholly on corn meal. In Erasmus Darwin's *Zoönomia* were interesting cases of mental derangement. This subject brought renewed interest in Dr. Benjamin Rush's theories and paved the way for *Wieland*. The writings of Godwin, Condorcet, Thomas

Paine, and other liberal political thinkers were read and reread, discussed and rediscussed, until each point was accepted or rejected.

In a sense this visit provided the direction in reading and thinking which a college education might have supplied more simply and more adequately six to ten years earlier. From this time a clearer, firmer intellectual command marked the pursuit of ideas. A new awareness of the relationship between literature and social action emerged from the examples given by Godwin's *Caleb Williams*, Robert Bage's novels, Mary Wollstonecraft's essays on women's rights, and Helen Maria Williams' letters on France. The path ahead had been cleared of some of the tangled underbrush, and the once distant goal now loomed on the horizon.

· 8 ·

Alcuin, "Sky-Walk," &
"The Man at Home"

AT HOME in Philadelphia after March 16, 1797, Brown subsided into old ways as if unaltered by a seven-month absence. Neglected was the formality of writing letters to the men in New York, friends whose kindness deserved at least a perfunctory note. Smith as usual chided the silent romancer, but removed the sting from his remarks by announcing a forthcoming visit with Dunlap to Philadelphia. From April 29 to May 10 the three friends again were together discussing animatedly such topics as courage, fortitude, intrepidity, and the superior merits of colonization over abolition as a solution to the problem of slavery. They visited the library to read a translation of Bürger's "Leonora"; Dunlap thought this "bewildered dream of a heart-broken girl ending in death finely imagined and executed." At Lailson's French equestrian circus they were oppressed by the uncomfortable thought of being part of an audience "pretending to rationality, yet sitting hour after hour to see men and women in fool's coats display the gambols of the monkey as the highest attainment of their persevering industry." Ashamed, the moralists tiptoed out before the performance ended. The trio went to see the new federal frigate being built in the shipyards, to call upon William Cobbett, to walk through William Bartram's botanical garden, and to attend a musical evening at Mrs. Levy's, where the two little Butler girls played the pianoforte.

Silence again dropped a curtain between the friends for nearly two months. "I have expected to hear from you till I have become sick of expectation," wrote Smith from New York on July 10. "Were I of a careless revengeful temper, I might let you go on in silence, and with like indifference cease all communication. But I have something to propose which may be worthy your attention, and I cannot find in my heart to hold my tongue." Again the younger man was energetic in his friend's behalf. Smith was maneuvering Brown into a position to require regular, systematic composition as a newspaper columnist.

Newspapers supplied the best opportunity for literary activity in the 1790's. Men with itching elbows might scribble a few paragraphs weekly to lend originality to a four-page paper composed largely of local advertisements, foreign intelligence copied from oversea newspapers, and official documents emanating from the capitol. Now and again an editor like Philip Freneau or Noah Webster wrote excellent essays on all manner of topics pertaining to the public welfare. In the larger communities lawyers and preachers frequently contributed periodical essays in imitation of Addison, Johnson, or Goldsmith. Dozens of such series ran the gamut of American intellectual striving in the first decade of the new country's history.

Joseph Dennie, a Harvard graduate, had made a mild stir by issuing a series of moralizing essays in book form under the title of *The Lay Preacher*. Called to the editorship of the Walpole, New Hampshire, *Farmer's Weekly Museum*, he requested assistance in the preparation of a column. Smith gained the impression, mistakenly no doubt, that pay would be given for contributions. Although he himself was unwilling to become "a dribbler and scribbler" for a country newspaper, Smith saw in the invitation an opportunity for Brown, to whom a letter was dispatched at once: "What think you of contributing a weekly essay to this miscellany? . . . I think it very probable that Dennie would willingly make pecuniary remuneration for assistance of this kind, regularly afforded, especially if the compensation were moderate and within his means." A prompt response indicated that the opportunity was to the Philadelphian's liking.

"I have a friend," wrote Smith to Dennie on July 24, 1797, "who is very capable of enriching your paper by original composition. He has both taste and learning, and is accustomed to compose. But he is poor, absolutely destitute. His pen is his only support, and he chiefly employs it mechanically." What justification there was for this remark about poverty in a clerkship remains in doubt, for at no time was Brown without funds. In New York both Brown and Smith lived economically; Brown acted as if he had no use for money, while Smith, systematically calculating his resources, contracted his wants rigidly within his means. Philosophically the Quaker had come to view money as the root of all evil; he scorned its use. Yet his attitude came not from poverty but from affluence. Dennie remained silent concerning the employment of a regular contributor despite a renewal of the suggestion, so that this plan necessarily was dropped.

As a sample of the type of essay to be contributed to the *Farmer's Museum,* Brown forwarded to Smith early in August the first two parts of *Alcuin,* a dialogue on the rights of women. This evidence of activity evoked pleasant responses in New York. At the homes of the physician's friends it was read aloud. "There is much truth, philosophical accuracy, and handsome writing in the essay," said Dunlap. Mrs. Seth Johnson, commending particularly the style, thought that in spite of the interesting statements on either side of the debate the ultimate design lacked clarity; she inferred that the object of *Alcuin* was to render women satisfied with their civil condition. Smith did not relish some of the sentiments. Yet such was his ambition to launch the young writer upon a career that, though still dependent upon his father, Smith at his own expense published the essay in a seventy-seven-page book on April 27, 1798. Meanwhile, the unstable author gave *Alcuin* to the Philadelphia *Weekly Magazine,* wherein Part I and a portion of Part II were printed under the title, "The Rights of Women." Smith at once enjoined serial publication, because the second version differed only in the substitution of the name "Edwin" for "Alcuin" and in some thirty minor stylistic alterations.

On receiving the manuscript of Parts III and IV on April 19, Smith noted in his diary: "They merit my applause, but I hesitate on the expediency of the publication. I must determine this doubt by a reference to a decision of a woman, one or more, unaccustomed to such speculations and ignorant of the author, but who has good sense and candor. Her advice shall be conclusive—at least for the present." A postscript was inserted in the little book to notify the public that Parts III and IV, although much longer, would be issued on the same terms as Parts I and II. Because of unfavorable comments the manuscript remained unprinted until Dunlap assembled his biography of Brown.

Alcuin is not really a dialogue; it begins as fiction, and only after some vacillation does it settle into the dialogue form. It opens with a biographical portrait of Alcuin, a respectable schoolmaster of limited means and social experience, who has been invited by Dr. Waring to join a circle of friends. The conversation proceeds from politics to the theme of woman's rights. Mrs. Carter, a widowed sister of the host, rebuts Alcuin's statement that woman's place is in the home; she declares that the exclusion of women from higher education prevents their preparing for admission to the learned professions. The schoolmaster is sure that "the assistance of a college is not necessary." She, however, proposes the establishment of coeducational colleges or, if objections are raised on the score of delicacy, the foundation of colleges in which both professors and students are female. To the segregation of the sexes in education she traces the loss by married women of all right to separate ownership of property.

"The tendency of rational improvement," she declares, "is to equalize conditions, to abolish all distinctions but those that are founded in truth and reason, to limit the reign of brute force and uncontrollable accidents. Women have unquestionably benefited by the progress that has hitherto taken place. If I look abroad, I may see reason to congratulate myself on being born in this age and country. . . . Perhaps there is no country in the world where the yoke is lighter than here. But this persuasion . . . ought not to blind us to our true condition." Alcuin then draws a generalized picture of the felicitous state of women and declares that, even in the poorest class, women have a better lot than men. The real question, Mrs. Carter says, is: "Are women as high in the scale of social felicity and usefulness as they may be and ought to be?" Alcuin admits that the answer must be negative, for, he says in closing Part I, "Human beings, it is to be hoped, are destined to a better condition on this stage, or some other, than is now allotted them." In Part II Mrs. Carter declaims warmly against the inequality and injustice of excluding women from voting and from office-holding. Alcuin confesses to prejudice against seeing a woman as President or Senator, but he offers the opinion that "in some respects women are superior to men."

Parts III and IV, printed without separation by Dunlap, contain a discussion of marriage and divorce. Mrs.

Carter, though fully aware of the new ideas on marriage, expresses disapproval, not of the institution in its entirety, but of the restrictive patterns by which "it renders the female a slave to man" and leaves the woman destitute of property. "The idea of common property is absurd and pernicious; but even this is better than poverty and dependence to which the present system subjects the female." "Marriage is sacred," she continues, "but iniquitous laws, by making it a compact of slavery, by imposing impracticable conditions and extorting impious promises, have in most countries converted it into something flagitious and hateful."

"Would you grant," inquires Alcuin, "an unlimited power of divorces?" "Without the least doubt," is the reply. "What shadow of justice is there in restraining mankind in this particular? My liberty is precious, but of all the ways in which my liberty can be infringed and my actions be subjected to force, heaven deliver me from this species of constraint." Alcuin replies, "Perhaps if entire liberty in this respect were granted, the effects might constitute a scene unspeakably more disastrous than anything hitherto conceived." He advances the argument that a general good must not be endangered by remedying a specific evil. Mrs. Carter reviews examples of marital unhappiness, indicates that wisdom does not always join with love, and asserts that "constancy is meritorious only within certain limits."

To Alcuin's query about the duty owed to children by parents, Mrs. Carter replies that children can be as happy in a divorced home as in one where nerves

are frayed by quarrelsomeness. Even in divorce the
parental relation continues, and the children are eligible to property settlements. Will chastity of mind
perish, asks Alcuin, if divorce be unlimited? No, she
replies, "Liberty, in this respect, would eminently
conduce to the happiness of mankind."

Alcuin now avers that "marriage has no other criterion than custom. This term is descriptive of that
mode of sexual intercourse, whatever it may be, which
custom or law has established in any country." The
question is, therefore, "What are the principles that
ought to regulate sexual intercourse?" Also, "What
conduct is incumbent upon me, when the species of
marriage established among my countrymen does not
conform to my notions of duty?" Mrs. Carter refuses to be carried into further heretical statements
and concludes by stating her position: "Marriage is
an union founded on free and mutual consent. It cannot exist without personal fidelity. As soon as it ceases
to be spontaneous, it ceases to be just."

Although Mrs. Carter has the last word in this discussion, the sentiments attributed to her inadequately
present the case for improved conditions. No idea is
dealt with conclusively or effectively. The young schoolmaster knows too little and skips mental rope too
rapidly. As a consequence *Alcuin* did little to stir
public discussion or to advance the cause of woman's
rights. Nor did the writing give evidence that the
author had made much progress on the road toward
giving shape to his liberal opinions. Well might readers
like Mrs. Seth Johnson inquire whether the claims of
women had been exhibited merely to have them ridi-

culed and thus to have further barriers placed in the path of reformers.

Among the many new plans formulated by Brown during a busy summer in 1797 was the writing of another novel. In September a hint indicated that such a work was in progress, but further information was not given. The strange kinks in Brown's mind were not ironed out. The old self-centered mode of life had been resumed. The friends in New York looked in vain for letters. As the months passed and as the wonder grew at this undeserved silence, Smith on November 30, 1797, chided his friend with a single-line letter: "Charles! Are you dead?" Not until New Year's Day did letters go forth. The one to Dunlap is an amazing document of uncharitable complaint and unwarranted self-condemnation; there had been no correspondence between them since they parted in Philadelphia on May 10. They had taken each other's friendship for granted during the years of their acquaintance. Possibly a fit of the blue devils akin to that which had aroused Smith on May 7, 1796, gave rise to this outburst on January 1, 1798:

It is nearly twelve months since I parted from you. I believe I have not written to you nor you written to me since. How shall I account for your silence? The task is an easy one. I was not an object of sufficient importance to justify the trouble. My infirmities and follies were too rooted for you to hope their cure. Admonition and remonstrance under your hand would be superfluous to this end. Hence your habitual reserve and silence of the pen suffered no interruption on my account. I lived with you six months. During that time you no doubt scrutinized my conduct and character with accuracy. You must have formed some conclusions respecting me, but you thought proper to be silent respecting them. You weighed the opposite advantages of communication and reserve. You decided in favor of the latter. I revere your rectitude, my friend, in as great a degree as I detest my own imbecility; but it is allowable for me to question the propriety of your decision.

Communication, it appears to me, was your duty. Whatever was my depravity, it did not sink me below deserving a mere verbal effort for my restoration. Had I led the way you would have followed. There needed only an introduction of the topic by me. Had I mentioned my opinion of your incommunicative temper and importuned you for a knowledge of your sentiments, the barrier would have been removed. It is true I was criminal in failing to employ this means. Were you exempt from blame in making these means necessary? Think of this, my friend, if I may still call you by that name. Surely, all esteem for me has not perished in your bosom.

I have never written to you. This is of a piece with the reserve of my conversation.

I think upon the life of last winter with self-loathing almost insupportable. I sometimes wish they were buried in oblivion, but even a wish of this kind is a token of my intellectual infirmity. Alas! my friend, few consolations of a self-approving mind have fallen to my lot. I have been raised to a sublimer pitch of speculation only to draw melancholy from the survey of the contrast between what I am and what I ought to be. I am sometimes apt to think that few human beings have drunk so deeply of the cup of self-abhorrence as I have. There is no misery equal to that which flows from this source. I have been for some years in the full fruition of it. Whether it will end but with my life I know not.

I have written to Elihu and informed him of the transactions of the last few months. You will of course be made acquainted with them. I know not whether your engagements have allowed you to prosecute any similar undertaking. What a dead and absolute vacuity has diffused itself between us! Not an event however momentous, which may have happened to you, is known to me. I have longed for a knowledge of your views and situation. I am not entitled to know them but by second hand. I make no demand upon you. As I am, you despise me. How can I remove the burden of your scorn but by transforming myself into a new being. I looked not forward to such a change. I shall die, as I have lived, a victim to perverse and incurable habits. My progress in knowledge has enlightened my judgment without adding to my power.

I have done nothing to deserve the esteem of your wife. I do not therefore expect it. That is no reason why I should refuse her my respect. She is in the highest degree entitled to it; present it therefore to her.

C. B. BROWN

Dunlap did not acknowledge this letter, but he wrote on the manuscript this regretful comment: "So at certain moments could think and write one of the purest and best beloved of men."

The letter to Smith, evidently more cheerful, announced the completion on the last day of December of the novel *Sky-Walk*, based upon Indian atrocities and upon somnambulism, one of the oddities of human behavior to which the physician had called attention. "I rejoice at the proofs you have at length attained to and exhibited of perseverance, industry, and success," wrote Smith in reply; "henceforth I dare to augur—timidly, I confess—better things of you."

Alcuin, &c.

Some promise of better things appeared in a letter printed in the Philadelphia *Weekly Magazine* of March 17, 1798:

You will be good enough to inform your readers that, in a short time, their patronage will be solicited to a work in which it is endeavored to amuse the imagination and improve the heart. . . . Our ecclesiastical and political system, our domestic and social maxims are in many respects entirely our own. He, therefore, who paints not from books but from nature, who introduces those lines and hues in which we differ rather than those in which we resemble our kindred nations beyond the ocean, may lay some claim to the patronage of his countrymen.

The value of such works lies without doubt in their moral tendency. The popular tales have their merit, but there is one thing in which they are deficient. They are generally adapted to one class of readers only. By a string of well-connected incidents they amuse the idle and thoughtless, but are spurned at by those who are satisfied with nothing but strains of lofty eloquence, the exhibition of powerful motives, and a sort of audaciousness of character. The world is governed not by the simpleton but by the man of soaring passions and intellectual energy. By the display of such only can we hope to enchain the attention and ravish the souls of those who study and reflect. To gain their homage it is not needful to forego the approbation of those whose circumstances have hindered them from making the same progress. A contexture of facts capable of suspending the faculties of every soul in curiosity may be joined with depth of views into human nature and all the subtleties of reasoning. Whether these properties be wedded in the present performance, the impartial reader must judge.

The writer is a native and resident of this city. Some part of his tale is a picture of truth. Facts have supplied the foundation of the whole. Its title is "Sky-Walk; or, The Man Unknown to Himself—An American Tale."

Another issue of the magazine explains the title: "Sky-Walk is a popular corruption of Ski-Wakkee, or Big Spring, the name given by the Lenni Lennaffee Indians to the district where the principal scenes of this novel are transacted." Actually the Algonquian words *ski wakkee* mean "fresh earth or new ground," and "Sky-Walk" is a folk adaptation of the Indian sounds in English ears. The subtitle indicates that some abnormality, possibly sleepwalking, marks the hero's life. A specimen chapter of the novel, printed in the *Weekly Magazine* of March 24, 1798, deals with the themes of benevolence and imprisonment for debt. The unmarried narrator tries to hide from his patroness the plight of his friend Annesley. This young Dublin merchant, whom the narrator met while traveling in France with Ormond Courtney, has been joint security with his father on a large debt; the debtor absconds, and the Annesleys are requested to make good their endorsements. The father dies, and the whole debt falls upon the shoulders of the younger man. Unable to pay, Annesley is imprisoned. When the patroness learns of his character, she directs the narrator to pay the debt and to transfer to Annesley an estate which places him "in a situation little inferior to that which his fancy had sketched as the summit of his wishes."

In April, Brown carried the manuscript of *Sky-*

Walk to New York, where Smith immediately took charge of bringing it to the attention of members of the Friendly Club. It was read aloud at meetings and social gatherings. Dunlap thought it "a very superior performance." Smith was enchanted at this new testimony of Brown's ability: "It has inexpressibly interested me. My whole spirit was affected by it." William Johnson retired to bed one evening before completing the book "in a throb and tumult of curiosity, interest, and admiration."

An unusual sequence of incidents prevented the publication of *Sky-Walk*. The manuscript was in James Watters' possession when the epidemic ravaged Philadelphia in 1798, and apparently some of the book was set in type. Watters died of yellow fever. The executors refused to complete the job or to sell the sheets of the finished portion at a reasonable price. The partially printed book was destroyed. Brown decided against issuing the novel through another publisher on the ground that *Sky-Walk* could be used to better advantage in other works. There is an element of prodigality in the way Brown cast his manuscripts to the winds. Smith had issued a reprimand in regard to this matter on July 24, 1797: "You have too low a sense of the value of reputation. You do not seem to regard how great may be its instrumentality in promoting the cause of truth. You are, therefore, faultily negligent to obtain praise; and your powers slumber unemployed."

James Watters' brief career as a publisher began with the establishment of *The Weekly Magazine of Original Essays, Fugitive Pieces, and Interesting In-*

telligence on February 3, 1798. Having supervised the printing of the American edition of the *Encyclopædia*, he set up independently as a printer-publisher with the ambition to give the United States a periodical of enduring value. To this end manuscripts were solicited from the educators and preachers in Philadelphia. Greatly excited about the venture, Brown emptied his portfolio and permitted Watters to use whatever seemed serviceable. Each issue, except one, between February 3 and August 25, 1798, contained a portion of at least one book by Brown. These excerpts included thirteen installments of "The Man at Home," the announcement and specimen chapter of *Sky-Walk*, seven installments of "A Series of Original Letters," nine chapters of *Arthur Mervyn*, and "The Rights of Women" which Smith was printing under the title of *Alcuin*. The young writer had enough manuscripts, apparently, to provide the new magazine with abundant and varied materials.

In these writings it is possible to trace Brown's development from a desultory essayist to a perfecter of tight fictional plots. Although the actual date and sequence of composition now cannot be determined, the way in which one work contributed to another serves adequately for a genetic study. It must be remembered that *Wieland* was published in September, 1798; *Ormond* on February 15, 1799; *Arthur Mervyn*, Part I, on May 21, 1799; and *Edgar Huntly* in August, 1799. Besides writing these novels, Brown undertook to edit *The Monthly Magazine and American Review*, the first, or April, issue of which came from the press on May 15, 1799. Parts of his earlier writings were lifted bodily into the four distinguished novels which were published within the space of eleven months. Never before had an American imaginative writer published as much fiction of high quality in so short a time.

"The Man at Home" narrates the thoughts and experiences of an unnamed elderly man who hides in the home of a Philadelphia laundress to escape imprisonment because he had signed the promissory notes of a defaulting friend. Apparently the essays of John Howard, the British reformer, had led Brown to write something about the injustice of imprisonment for debt. Unhappily the novelist knew all too little about this subject, for in the end the narrator, wearied of his self-imposed confinement, surrenders to the sheriff and goes to jail. Punishment is justified "inasmuch as it tends to prevent the destruction of life and the infringement of property." Again the moralist relinquished Godwinian notions and joined the conservative side in a vexed contemporary social question. More interesting, however, than the narrator's own experiences are those of the De Moivre family, an episode of which was inserted as the seventh chapter of *Ormond*. The only significant alteration in this account of a daughter burying her father at night during the plague was the change of the family name to Monrose.

"A Series of Original Letters" is the beginning of an epistolary novel in which a young law student in Philadelphia becomes acquainted with the bold schemes of Beddoes and with the seemingly immoral activities of Beddoes' secretive sister, Lucy. There are close parallels in incident between this work and *Arthur Mervyn;* in each the hero ferrets out the misdeeds of a cunning villain, and a house of prostitution plays a decisive part in the life of the heroine. The concealed brother-sister relationship appears again in *Ormond* in the connection between Ormond and Martinette de Beauvais.

Although these works lack firm structure and only occasionally show flashes of the aphoristic quality of the four meritorious novels, it is apparent that the once shapeless sentences are taking the unmistakable form of bullets speeding directly to their mark. The faults of expository generalization and of too highly compressed narrative are here. The stories sweep along too rapidly; there seldom is sufficient description and conversation to give an air of verisimilitude. Yet these trial efforts taught Brown how to create suitable characters and to formulate well-motivated plots. The basic principles in his philosophy of fiction were emerging clearly, and he phrased some of them in a bit of advice given to Miss De Moivre in regard to her proposed autobiography:

You aspire to the station of a moralist. The scope of your wishes is to free your own sex from servitude and folly. How shall this be done? By writing. But what shall you write? . . . Sit down to the detailing of your own adventures and the portraying of your own character.

Search as widely as you will; turn over all the annals of illustrious females: there is none in whom you shall find a rival to yourself. In the selection of the subjects of useful history, the chief point is not the virtue of a character. The prime regard is to be paid to the genius and force of mind that is displayed. Great energy employed in the promotion of vicious purposes constitutes a very useful spectacle. Give me a tale of lofty crimes rather than of honest folly. In this respect the history of your own country [France] is not barren. What think you of Katherine de Medici? Or to ascend somewhat higher, what think you of Joan d'Arc? . . . Subtlety in invention of causes, fertility in the invention, judgment in the arrangement, and eloquence in exhibiting the facts would constitute a precious scene.

·9·

Wieland;
or, The Transformation

DURING the autumn and winter of 1797-1798
Brown fell in love with Miss Susan A. Potts, a young
Philadelphian about whom no information survives.
On March 29, 1798, Smith showed Dunlap a letter
in which Brown described himself as assiduously writing
novels and in love. Late in April Miss Potts visited
New York City. After calling to pay his respects,
Smith reported: "Without being beautiful, she is very
interesting. Our talk was on common topics, as there
was a third person present, but it evinced good sense.
All that I see is in her favor." Parental objection to
their marriage, possibly because Miss Potts was not a
Quaker, caused relations to be broken off forcibly.
On occasion the novelist made light of his lovelorn
state, but without doubt his feelings had been rudely
shocked by the attitude of his family, particularly that

of his mother whose intervention finally forced the issue.

On July 3, 1798, Brown arrived in New York City for another of his extended visits. His health was pretty well restored, although his spirits flagged at thoughts of the unkind tactics of his family. For nine days he resided with Dunlap; then on July 12 he moved into the quarters of Smith and Johnson at 45 Pine Street.

Johnson's law practice had increased extensively because of the rage for speculation in Western lands, the purchase of foreign notes, and litigation relating to contracts. Smith's medical practice had grown, partly because of connections made at the hospital and partly because of favorable public interest in the *Medical Repository*. Physicians recognized his attainments by calling him as a consultant. Brown, alone during much of the day, was free to concentrate upon the completion of his projects. At leisurely breakfasts and dinners the three men ran over the ground of their many interests; each day brought new schemes for doing good. They worried over Seth and Horace Johnson, whose business was on the verge of bankruptcy. In Philadelphia, Joseph Bringhurst, Jr., had suffered imprisonment for debt as a result of unfortunate business commitments. Knowing the integrity of these friends, the three roommates worried less about them than about laws which permitted egregious wrongs. The ground of their religious beliefs was retraced, but Johnson refused to go the whole road in renouncing orthodox Christianity. Brown was testing theological ideas in *Wieland;* the more he wrote the less certain he was of the attainment of a simple solution of complicated psychological and social problems.

The triumvirate moved about the city as a unit in social visits to the homes of Roulet, Seth and Horace Johnson, the two Millers, Dr. Mitchill, Boyd, Templeton, Riley, Lovegrove, Charles Adams, Moses Rogers, General Hughes, and William and Gurdon Woolsey. Almost daily the three friends visited Dunlap or he visited them. At these houses as guests were some of the most distinguished men of the day. Timothy Dwight, Yale's president, stopped by frequently. General Bloomfield crossed the river from New Jersey to meet New York friends. Albert Gallatin occasionally came to the city to look after political interests as well as to complete business matters concerned with his manufacturing activities in the Monongahela River Valley. Noah Webster on a research tour requested critical comments upon the first chapter of *A Brief History of Epidemic Diseases*. Jedidiah Morse, preacher and geographer, was carrying on a crusade against the Illuminati, a European subversive order with some few adherents in America. Hints for *Ormond* were derived from this pugnacious fundamentalist. Statesmen from New England lingered a day or two in New York in passing to and from the capitol in Philadelphia; Senator Uriah Tracy of Connecticut had been especially friendly in introducing political leaders. Yet no other event seemed quite so notable this summer as the appearance, on July 27, of President John Adams. A military company paraded its maneuvers from early morning until his arrival at five P.M. The three friends waited at the Battery all day to meet the national leader who was the father of their intimate companion.

Into one other organization Brown was drawn on July 16, 1798. In company with Smith, William Johnson, and Samuel Miles Hopkins, he went to Dr. Samuel Latham Mitchill's rooms at Columbia College, where, in addition to the host, they found Dr. Edward Miller and the Reverend Samuel Miller. After some discussion the group founded the American Mineralogical Society. In addition to those present at the meeting, the following were admitted as charter members: William Dunlap; Solomon Simpson, a Jewish merchant; and George J. Warner, a watchmaker.

At breakfast on August 7, Smith, Johnson, Dunlap, and Brown talked over the project of bringing out through T. and J. Swords a weekly magazine. The success of the *Medical Repository*, issued by the same printers, augured well for a literary paper, especially if the novelist were to take charge. Before active work could be begun, yellow fever again terrified the city, and the dynamic leader of the group had fallen victim.

The Friendly Club had discontinued meeting after the normal attendance in May dwindled to one or two members besides the three roommates. In a sense the American Mineralogical Society replaced the earlier club, although Mitchill held the new group quite rigorously to a discussion of scientific matters. Brown trailed Smith to these meetings; there is no evidence that the busy novelist devoted himself seriously to a study of the classification or chemical analysis of rocks. Recognizing the need for companionship, Brown merely went along with Smith and Johnson; at this time he did not strike out for himself to create friends of his own.

Brown brought to New York, as evidence of enthusiasm for novel writing, the first pages of a new book. In Philadelphia on April 12, 1798, he had read to Dunlap "the beginning to a novel undertaken since *Sky-Walk;* he calls it *Wieland; or, The Transformation.* This must make a very fine book." On July 3 Dunlap noted further: "C. B. Brown arrives from Philadelphia—last from Princeton—and takes up his abode with me. He has brought his second novel but not completed." The little circle of intimates passed the manuscript around. Smith found it "no way inferior to *Sky-Walk.*" By July 10 eighty-four pages of manuscript had been completed. Smith took this packet to Hocquet Caritat, bookseller and owner of New York's fashionable circulating library, who purchased the rights to the novel. On July 23 copy was sent to the printer, T. and J. Swords. Having received fifty dollars as an initial payment, Brown hurried to a conclusion to keep pace with the typesetters. On August 5 the novel was completely written, although some additions and alterations in the proof were made as late as August 24. The book was published on September 14, 1798, and put on sale at a dollar a copy.

Wieland; or, The Transformation is a terror story in which the narrator, the beautiful Clara Wieland, is driven toward madness by a series of shivering experiences, is rescued at the end, and is allowed to complete her gloom-clouded life in marriage. She is the daughter of a German-born religious fanatic who has come to America as a missionary and who has

foretold his death by strange, unannounced means of
retribution for supposed lax service to God. With
trembling joints and chattering teeth he goes one sultry August midnight, in customary solitude, to worship in a private chapel on his estate. Half an hour
later his wife notices a gleam of light in the chapel.
There follows a loud report like the explosion of an
undersea bomb. Piercing shrieks seem to be a call for
help. The blaze resembles a cloud impregnated with
light, but the building is not on fire. Brought to his
bed, the fanatic states that while engaged in silent
prayers he was disturbed by a faint gleam of light in
the chapel as if someone carried a lamp. On turning
to look at the supposed intruder, he was struck on
the right arm by a club. A bright spark fell on him,
and in a moment his clothes were burned to ashes.
Wieland dies by spontaneous combustion, exactly in
the manner of the priest Don G. Maria Bertholi, as
described in the London *Literary Magazine* of May,
1790. But the question is raised by Clara whether this
event is "fresh proof that the Divine Ruler interferes
in human affairs" or is the natural consequence of
"the irregular expansion of the fluid that imparts
warmth to our heart and blood, caused by the fatigue
of the preceding day, or flowing by established laws
from the condition of his thoughts."

It is against this background of religious mania and
of imagined supernatural intervention in the affairs
of men that the main story is related. Clara and her
brother Theodore, who are about seven and ten years
old, respectively, when their father dies, are reared
by a maiden aunt under circumstances of affluence.

Wieland's studious habits and musical interests arise from a humorless, melancholy disposition. The history of religion and the textual accuracy of Cicero are his favorite studies. Neither child has been able to forget the terrifying childhood experience, and almost every significant incident clangs the bell of memory to renew the indelible impact of that tragic occurrence. The story proper begins six years after Theodore has married Catharine Pleyel and after four children have been born to this union.

Like his father, Theodore is a religious enthusiast who imagines that he can have direct communication with God. The ardent Clara sees in almost every unmarried man a potential suitor; secretly she has nourished affection for Henry Pleyel, Catharine's brother, a rationalist engaged to the German baroness Theresa von Stolberg. One evening, as the four are conversing, Wieland goes to his father's chapel, now converted to a study and music hall, to find a letter. A mysterious voice warns him to return to the house. Seven times in the course of a few weeks the voice is heard under varying and increasingly mystifying circumstances. Wieland is certain of the supernatural origin of the voice, Clara thinks the voice is supernatural but not malevolent in intention, and Pleyel, who has been told of the death of his sweetheart in one of the voice's statements, wavers momentarily until his rationalistic tendency reasserts itself.

A stranger named Carwin, an escaped convict from Ireland with eyes and voice suggesting powers of witchcraft, comes into the family circle. On one occasion he appears in Clara's bedroom at midnight after the voice has been heard. He assures her that but for the supernatural protection afforded by the voice he would have seduced her. Pleyel, whose affection has centered on Clara, witnesses Carwin's departure from her room and turns angrily against her because of her seemingly profligate conduct.

Wieland goes mad under the strain of the circumstances and, because he thinks he hears a divine command, strangles his wife and children and bashes in the head of Louisa Stuart, a young girl living with the Wielands. His attempt on Pleyel's life fails. Carwin suddenly appears and explains his ventriloquial powers just as Wieland menaces Clara. Aware of his error, Wieland grasps her penknife, with which she intended to slay him, and plunges the blade to the hilt in his own neck.

Three years later Clara resumes the narrative. Theresa is dead in childbirth. Pleyel, having learned the truth about Clara's innocence, marries her. The story of Louisa Stuart's parents is briefly concluded as a parallel narrative leading to an identical moralized conclusion. Stuart had wounded Maxwell in a duel, and in revenge Maxwell had seduced Stuart's wife. When Stuart learns of his wife's self-exile in shame, he pursues Maxwell to secure revenge. A challenge is issued, but at night Stuart is murdered by an unknown swarthy assassin. This briefly narrated secondary story is designed to give point to the lesson that "the evils of which Carwin and Maxwell were the authors owed their existence to the errors of the sufferers." If Mrs. Stuart had crushed her disastrous passion, and if Stuart had not sought an "absurd revenge," the catastrophe would not have occurred. If Wieland had framed juster notions of moral duty and if Clara had been gifted with ordinary equanimity or foresight, the double-tongued Carwin would not have ensnared them.

This conclusion has an anticlimactic force, since the scene shifts from the Wieland family to the Stuart family. Though esthetically the episode cannot be justified today, to the story-telling moralist in 1798 it helped to give a ring of truth, for dueling and seduction were frowned upon. The parallel between common and uncommon experiences heightens the necessity for a rationalistic examination of evidence before one draws conclusions or engages in actions likely to destroy life or happiness.

The novel has other defects. Conversation occurs too seldom, and then chiefly in Wieland's confession. Most of the episodes are summarized too briefly. Description tends to be general and expository rather than pictorial. Opportunities for magnificent scenes are not exploited; a notable example is the comment following the discovery of the bodies of the five murdered children: "Why should I protract a tale which I already begin to feel is too long?" This episode of a religious maniac's murder of his family expands an account, as related in the New York *Weekly Magazine* of July 20, 1796, of James Yates' murder of his whole family in Tomhanick, New York, in December, 1791.

The virtues of the novel are numerous. The main story moves with steady crescendo to a powerful climax. It is, as Thomas Love Peacock said, "one of the few tales in which the final explanation of the apparently supernatural does not destroy or diminish the original effect." The reader is so engrossed in the plight of the narrator, Clara, since she is under threat throughout, that the explanation by Carwin of his cunning serves but to increase the danger to Clara's mental balance and life. Brown organized his story, unlike most Gothic tales, around the theme of mental balance and the ease with which that balance is destroyed. The pseudo-supernatural materials, spontaneous combustion and ventriloquism, serve to make credible Theodore's insanity. Clara is prostrated at two periods, and in the presence of Carwin she faints twice. She possesses a hereditary dread of water. Her education, she says, did not fit her for perils such as she encounters. In the moralizing conclusion, therefore, she advises the necessity for maintaining one's balance through a rationalistic attitude towards all phenomena.

The plot unfolds skillfully. The initial chapters set the somber, tragic mood of the tale; ever present in the minds of Clara and Theodore, and used advantageously by Carwin, are the events of the elder Wieland's fiery death; that episode chimes in the memory like a knell, horrifyingly symbolical of a dread, inevitable catastrophe. The small cast of characters, closely interknit through marriage and affection, as well as through the proximity of their residences to each other and to the city of Philadelphia, makes plausible each turn of the action. Clara's penknife appears early as a weapon of defense, and at last serves its tragic purpose in Theodore's hand. Every detail of the main story is adequately motivated.

The unfolding of the tale from three angles evinces masterly command of plot structure. After Clara has narrated the events from her point of view, Theodore confesses to the court, and finally Carwin unravels the mystery. Each flickering light and each of the seven appearances of the ventriloquial voice is accounted for. If Brown managed the dovetailing of these three reports less artfully than recent writers of detective fiction have done, it should be remembered that he was pioneering in a field where Poe, thirty years later, is credited with originality. Brown anticipated Hawthorne in the use of multiple explanation of seemingly supernatural events.

It is often erroneously assumed that Theodore is the central character in the novel. The story revolves about the narrator, Clara, a young woman of exceptional mentality, fortitude, loyalty, and frankness. She begins by asking attention to her own plight, "a destiny without alleviation." She worries over the supernatural agency of the voices; she sighs for a lover and unhesitatingly reveals her hopes; she who had spurned Dashwood on an earlier occasion feels the menace of a practiced seducer in a series of midnight actions, the unhappy result of which is the temporary loss of her hoped-for husband, Pleyel; she dreams of threats to her life and meditates upon their meaning; she stumbles upon the murdered Catharine and children; Theodore twice is within an inch of murdering her; and in the end she becomes the bride of Pleyel.

The subtitle of the novel, "The Transformation," occurs thrice in the text. It first describes Carwin's alteration from an Englishman into an Irishman. Clara next uses the term in relation to herself: "Was I not likewise transformed from rational and human into a

[*106*]

creature of nameless and fearless attributes?" Finally it describes Theodore: "Wieland was transformed at once into a *man of sorrows*." Although the word is not used directly about Pleyel, the description of his ineffable anguish on berating Clara for her alleged lapse from virtue indicates a similar "transformation." At the very beginning of the novel, in the third paragraph, Clara describes the transformation of the status of the whole family: "The storm that tore up our happiness and changed into dreariness and desert the blooming scene of our existence is lulled into grim repose, but not until the victim was transfixed and mangled, till every obstacle was dissipated by its rage, till every remnant of good was wrested from our grasp and exterminated." The title, which refers as much to the family as to Theodore, certainly must not be interpreted as excluding Clara from the central position.

Brown endowed his main characters with a sufficient variety of traits to make their friendship plausible and their actions credible. Although he drew his incidents and persons as much from books as from life, his emphasis upon psychopathic traits adds depth to characters whose range of action is narrow in the physical world. This intense intellectuality in *Wieland* gives it precedence in importance over almost all other early American novels. Quite apparent is Brown's indebtedness to contemporary sensationalist psychology, to Erasmus Darwin's chapter on "Mania Mutabilis" in *Zoönomia*, and to other writings on insanity. Dr. Cambridge's lecture to Clara echoes Dr. Benjamin Rush. Not until the advent of Poe and Hawthorne does another fictionist create characters tormented by brooding minds.

Not only in the psychological passages is *Wieland* a
vehicle of intellectuality. Everywhere are evidences
of learning. There has been research in religion, in
old books, in encyclopedias. A problem in emending
Cicero occupies some time of Theodore, who is an accomplished Latin textual scholar and a student of the
history of religion. These characters are children of
the Enlightenment. Each possesses utopian dreams.
Clara muses on methods to end the alliance between
the practice of agriculture and ignorance; she hopes
that "this trade might be made conducive to or at
least consistent with acquisition of wisdom and eloquence." Her heart is readily "touched with sympathy
for the children of misfortune." Pleyel, a possessor
of a skeptical mind in most matters, urges Theodore
to claim estates in Germany because wealth would
"afford so large a field for benevolence." Theodore
refuses, however, on the ground that wealth and power
are two great sources of depravity.

Brown's style emphasizes the intellectuality of the
novel. The vocabulary is large; the words are not
notably learned, although the tendency to employ poly-
syllables of Latin derivation is apparent: "My calmness was the torpor of despair, and not the tranquillity
of fortitude." Circumlocution replaces direct description: "he fell in love" becomes "he had not escaped
the amorous contagion." The uniqueness of Brown's
style lies in the short, rapid-fire sentences which can-
nonade the reader's mind with ideas faster than they
can be absorbed. Fiction should proceed pictorially;
Brown's story marches steadily forward under sen-
tentious garb as if he were vying with Rochefoucauld

or Pascal in the writing of the following aphorisms:

As a consolation in calamity religion is dear.

Some agitation and concussion is requisite to the due exercise of human understanding.

This scene of existence is, in all its parts, calamitous.

Ideas exist in our minds that can be accounted for by no established laws.

Surprise is an emotion that enfeebles, not invigorates.

Mankind are more easily enticed to virtue by example than by precept.

Terror enables us to perform incredible feats.

Time will obliterate the deepest impressions.

These sentences parallel similar ones in William Godwin's *Caleb Williams* and *An Enquiry into Political Justice*. But they also parallel statements in Robert Bage's *Hermsprong* and in other fiction of a liberal tendency. Although Brown had been reading Godwin and had despaired of surpassing this master in the first pages of *Arthur Mervyn*, he was not merely copying plot or ideas or style in *Wieland*. There are more similarities with Bage's novel than with Godwin's, for in Bage are the German characters, an octagonal pleasure house, a thirty-thousand-acre plantation of the type mentioned by Ludloe and Carwin, a nature-setting with a perpendicular descent, and a generally radical intellectual tendency. Brown also was familiar with Anne Radcliffe's novels of suspense wherein seemingly supernatural occurrences were explained away as natural phenomena. His descriptions and his use of the sex motif follow the pattern of her novels.

Of considerable interest in the history of fiction are the references to German characters and the use of German Gothic formulæ. The end of the eighteenth century saw a shift of British intellectual interests away from France because of the declaration of war in 1793. German exiles and men like Matthew Lewis and Henry MacKenzie turned attention to the hitherto unexploited literary production of Prussia. Christoph Martin Wieland (1773-1813) was being mentioned in the magazines with fulsome praise for his epic *Oberon* (1780), a work which Brown read in 1793. Here in the public eye was a man whose sensitivity gave plausibility to Theodore's possession of religious mania. Dunlap had translated Schiller's and Kotzebue's dramas, and the New York *Weekly Magazine* had serialized Schiller's *The Ghostseer* and Cajetan Tschink's *The Victim of Magical Delusion*. Brown had read these two novels, and possibly the initial creative impulse and rationalistic theme of *Wieland* came from the latter. Other German and English novels doubtless influenced Brown, but by and large *Wieland* is an original work in subject, theme, plot, and execution.

Despite its publication at the very height of the plague on September 15, 1798, the book received favorable attention. With the resumption of normal city life, the New York *Spectator* of November 10, 1798, extolled the book in a review nearly a column in length: "The style is correct and energetic, and we may venture to assert the writer has established his reputation as a man of genius." The reviewer called upon his fellow citizens to support the author: "On the reception of this volume depends the future exertions of this ingenious man. Shall it be said that America, whose citizens have been famed for their superior knowledge and love of letters, is so destitute of liberality as to refuse or neglect patronizing an attempt like the present? And shall this stigma in a particular manner rest upon our city? . . . Forbid it, patriotism; forbid it, all that has any connection with science [that is, learning] and the *Amor Patriæ*."

On January 2, 1799, another reviewer in the same newspaper stated: *"Wieland; or, The Transformation* . . . is certainly the best novel this country has produced. It is a work which no one can read with inattention, and is peculiarly engaging to well-cultivated and refined understandings. Every person, however well informed he may be, must find his curiosity gratified and his mind enlarged after a candid and judicious perusal of this ingenious performance. This is not the flimsy production of a wretched hireling or a mercenary garreteer, but the well-finished composition of one who may be truly called 'a man of genius.' In a word, I think we may with propriety assert that the writer of *Wieland* was desirous of producing a work from the perusal of which no one could rise without being strengthened in habits of sincerity, fortitude, and justice." In *The American Review and Literary Journal* of July-September, 1801, this statement was made: "The author of *Wieland* is almost the first American who has adventured in this path of literature, and this production is the first of the kind which has attracted much public attention." Caritat took copies with him to England, and brief critiques there were favorable.

Evidently the sale was not sufficient to call for a second edition immediately. Samuel Griswold Goodrich reprinted it in 1829 in a collected edition of the novels, and in 1841 W. Coquebert issued a French translation, *Wieland, ou la voix mystérieux.* Meantime, Hawthorne, Poe, and other critics praised Brown and *Wieland;* and since its first publication the book has been acclaimed a minor classic in American literature.

Something of Brown's tremulous concern over the fate of *Wieland* appears in a letter of December 25, 1798, to Thomas Jefferson: "In thus transmitting my book to you, I tacitly acknowledge my belief that it is capable of affording you pleasure and of entitling the writer to some portion of your good opinion. I . . . hope that an artful display of incidents, the powerful delineation of characters and the train of eloquent and judicious reasoning which may be combined in a fictitious work will be regarded by Thomas Jefferson with as much respect as they are regarded by me."

As soon as *Wieland* was completed, Brown resumed work on *Carwin, The Biloquist* which, he had announced in his preface to *Wieland,* would "be published or suppressed according to the reception which is given to the present attempt." *Carwin* never was completed; the surviving fragment was first printed in *The Literary Magazine and American Register* between 1803 and 1805.

Carwin, The Biloquist forms a preliminary volume to *Wieland,* much as the first part of Godwin's *Caleb Williams* describes the villain's career before the hero is introduced. Carwin, son of a western Pennsylvania farmer, possesses a curiosity like Caleb Williams'. At fourteen he becomes interested in ventriloquism through the operation of a five-fold echo in a glen. He succeeds in mimicking every species of sound, human and animal. Sent to live with an aunt in Philadelphia, he meets Ludloe, a wealthy Irishman and agrees to go to Europe.

Ludloe enunciates a strange code of conduct: he seems to be an anarchist; his talk savors of the subversive ideas of the Illuminati. He echoes Alcuin on the subject of the perverting nature of all professions, on the evils of cohabitation, and on the misguided thinking of women as a result of false principles of education. He believes that "the absurd and unequal distribution of property gave birth to poverty and riches" and that the evils which infest society are caused by the errors of opinion. A perfectionist, he believes further "that man is the creature of circumstances; that he is capable of endless improvement; that his progress has been stopped by the artificial impediment of government; that by the removal of this, the fondest dreams of imagination will be realized." Ludloe also has "a scheme of utopian felicity, where the empire of reason should supplant that of force; where justice should be universally understood and practiced; where the interest of the whole and of the individual should be seen by all to be the same; where the public good should be the scope of all activity; where the tasks of all should be the same, and the means of subsistence equally distributed."

Carwin while studying in Spain embraces Roman Catholicism. His correspondence with Ludloe leads to the exposition of a plan for a new nation to be established on the colonization principle of the manumission societies; he believes that men persist in retaining error because they are creatures of habit, and that in a new land "a new race, tutored in truth, may in a few centuries overflow the habitable world." Not until he arrives in Dublin does Carwin discover Ludloe's secret, but the novel breaks off before the two men come to open conflict. The sequel in *Wieland* accuses Carwin of murdering Lady Jane Conway and of robbing Ludloe—charges which Carwin claims are false.

Brown felt that his narrative was following too closely the pattern of *Caleb Williams* and of the beginning of *Arthur Mervyn,* already published in the Philadelphia *Weekly Magazine.* In abandoning his plan, he laid aside a swift-paced tale involving only a single strand of action. Carwin possesses little distinctiveness in character, and the conflict between him and Ludloe would have been difficult to manage on ideological or psychological grounds because both have similar utopian notions. No ideas are in conflict, and *Carwin* develops no theme of importance equal to that of *Wieland.* But where *Wieland* is almost wholly original, *Carwin* seems wholly derivative in pattern and character from Godwin. Though the verbal power remains, Brown correctly diagnosed the chief weakness of the novel when he wrote in 1805 that "the narrative [is] of too grave and argumentative a cast."

On September 4, 1798, Brown wrote to Dunlap: "I have written something in the history of Carwin, which I will send. I have deserted for the present from the prosecution of this plan, and betook myself to another which I mean to extend to the size of *Wieland* and to finish by the end of this month, provided no yellow fever disconcerts my plan." On the 24th, while he and Dunlap were together in Perth Amboy to escape the ravages of yellow fever, Dunlap noted in his diary: "Read the beginning of Charles' last novel called *Calvert* (proposed to be changed to *Caillemour*) or *The Lost Brothers*." This work, the first volume of an uncompleted pentalogy, was entitled *Memoirs of Stephen Calvert* and was first published serially in Brown's *Monthly Magazine and American Review* from June, 1799, to June, 1800; Dunlap reprinted it in his biography of Brown.

Death of Elihu Hubbard Smith

YELLOW FEVER had stricken the city of New York annually during the 1790's. Like hundreds of other cautious men who fled to rural areas during the infectious season, Dunlap removed to Perth Amboy. None of the three roommates deemed it necessary to withdraw from the city, because 45 Pine Street seemed out of the neighborhood usually infected. Smith's duties required that he remain, although many of the physicians, knowing their skill useless, hurried away at the announcement of the first case of yellow fever. In a letter to his brother James on August 25, 1798, Brown remarked: "Heavy rains, uncleansed sinks, and a continuance of unexampled heat have within these ten days given birth to the yellow fever among us in its epidemical form. Death and alarms have rapidly multiplied, but it is hoped that now, as formerly, its influences will be limited to one place. You may be under no concern on my account, since my abode is far enough from the seat of the disease, and my mode of living, from which animal food and spirituous liquors are wholly excluded, gives the utmost security."

On the 27th Smith was painfully bitten by mosquitoes; on this evening he was called from a sound slumber to visit a patient on Long Island. The trip across the ferry, the horseback ride to the patient's home, and the equally wearisome return journey undermined the physician's health. He complained of a bad cold and catarrh, of a run-down state which would open his body for the entrance of the fever. But the daily round of duties was continued until September 4, when a scorching fever drove him to bed. On the 7th, in spite of "perpetual tears and perpetual drizzling from the nose," he started forth again to prescribe at the hospital and to consult with other physicians.

Meanwhile Brown reported to his brother, who had urgently requested retreat to the country, that newspaper items had exaggerated the condition of the city. "There is abundance of alarm," he added, "and the streets most busy and frequented will speedily be evacuated. As to the malignity of this disease, perhaps its attack is more violent than ordinary, but E. H. S. . . . answers for me that not more than one out of nine when properly nursed dies, and that its fatality therefore is less than the same disease in Philadelphia. In the present healthful state of this neighborhood it would be absurd to allow fear to drive me away. When there is actual and indisputable danger, it would be no less absurd to remain, since, even if the disease terminate favorably or even were certain so to terminate, we are sure of being infinitely troublesome to others and of undergoing much pain." Adverting to Smith's illness, Brown continued: "E. H. S. has extensive and successful practice in this disease. Through fatigue and exposure to midnight airs he is at present somewhat indisposed, but will shortly do well. If when this fever attacks our neighborhood I run away, I am not sure that I shall do right. E. H. S. at least, probably Johnson, will remain; if I run the risk of requiring to be nursed, I must not forget that others may require to be nursed by me in a disease where personal attentions are all in all."

The lofty position here taken by Brown, that abstract justice required his remaining, was quite in accord with the principles being enunciated in his essays and novels. Repeated requests from his family that he retire to Burlington or to Connecticut were turned down. Their urgency had the effect of drawing letters almost daily from him. "The atmosphere is perceptibly different from former years," he wrote a few days later, "and leaves nobody in perfect health, but the quarter where I reside is still free from sickness. All the physicians who have attended patients in this fever have been indisposed. Our friend E. H. S.'s indisposition has nearly gone, but he ascribed his preservation from death entirely to his vegetable diet and his refusing his attendance at the beginning of his complaint to the summons of the sick. He is now nearly able to resume his medical functions. Five physicians much conversant with the sick have died within a very short space."

On September 11 the humane principles of the young physician were put to a practical test. Word came from the Tontine Coffee House that Dr. Joseph Scandella, freshly arrived from Philadelphia, had every symptom of the fever. Smith at once ordered the ailing visitor to be conveyed to 45 Pine Street; thus the dread disease was introduced into the apartment of the three friends.

Scandella, a Venetian, studied medicine two years while secretary to the Venetian Embassy in London. Upon learning the news of the extinction of the Venetian Republic by Napoleon on May 16, 1797, Scandella set out for the youthful empire in the West to see the republican form of government in successful operation. After a year of travel, principally through the South and West, he returned in August via Philadelphia to New York to embark for Europe. Through some mischance his baggage was delayed in Philadelphia, and, learning that dear friends there were ill of yellow fever, he retraced his footsteps only to be the unhappy witness of the deaths of those whom he desired to aid. Worn down with fatigue, he persisted in journeying to New York City. While crossing the marshes between Newark and the city he first felt the disease upon him. Smith's acquaintance with this cultivated stranger had been made only in August; when the boarding houses closed their doors to him, Scandella pleaded the ties of profession and of friendship in begging succor. To Smith's bed the Italian physician was immediately carried, and Smith became both physician and nurse, rising several times each night to attend the patient's calls.

On September 17 Brown described to his brother the events leading to Scandella's death and Smith's fatal illness:

When calamity is at a distance it affects us but little, and no sympathy for others can realize that distress which does not immediately affect us. You have discovered by the public papers the deplorable condition of our city, which in fact exceeds that of Philadelphia, inasmuch as the mortality bears a greater proportion to the population with us. Another circumstance greatly enhances our calamity, for the victims to this disease have been in innumerable cases selected from the highest and most respectable class of inhabitants. Till lately, horrible as this evil is, and much conversant with it through the medium of physicians as I had been, I was not much affected by it until, during the last week, this fatal pest has encompassed us and entered our own doors.

On Tuesday last an Italian gentleman of great merit and a particular friend of E. H. S. arrived in this city from Philadelphia. The disease had already been contracted, and admission into the boarding house was denied him. Hearing of his situation, our friend hastened to his succor and resigned to him his own bed. A nurse was impossible to be procured, and this duty therefore devolved upon us. The disease was virulent beyond example, but his agonies have been protracted to this day. He now lies in one compartment of our house, a spectacle that sickens the heart to behold, and not far from his last breath, while in the next our friend E. H. S. is in a condition but little better. Extreme fatigue and anxieties could not fail of producing a return of this illness in Elihu. How it will end Heaven knows.

Sunday evening. Our Italian friend is dead, and Elihu is preparing to be transported to Horace Johnson's, whose house is spacious, healthfully situated, and plentifully accommodated. Our own house is a theater of death and grief, where his longer continuance would infallibly destroy him and us. Before his last attack

E. H. S. became sensible of the disproportionate hazard which he incurred, and had determined, as soon as his friend Scandella had recovered or perished and his present patients had been gotten rid of, to withdraw from town.

Smith's "symptoms were peculiarly malignant," wrote Horace Johnson, "although to the inexperienced eye his indisposition appeared to be lassitude and the effect of uncommon fatigue and weariness. His attack was [marked by] vomiting and a slight pain in the back; and the same continued to death. No act or remedy could compose his stomach." Dr. Mitchill and Dr. Miller attended their fellow editor of the *Medical Repository;* they followed usual procedure in first bleeding the patient copiously and then in applying mercurial ointment generously over the whole body. Smith writhed at a cure more painful than the disease; enfeebled by the bloodletting, he sank into a stupor. His friends took him to Horace Johnson's home on Greenwich Street, where, after a violent spasm and nausea, he calmly resigned himself to death.

On the day before Smith's death Brown began a letter which throbbed with despair:

What shall I write? I know that you ought to have frequent information of what is passing here, but I cannot trust myself with the narrative. My labor is to forget and exclude surrounding scenes and recent incidents. Smith is not dead, but unless miracles be wrought for him, another day will number him with the victims of this most dreadful and relentless of pestilences. My excellent friend Dr. Miller dissuades me from going to you. The journey is long, and the consequence of falling sick upon the road may be easily conceived. Here then I must remain.

The number of physicians is rapidly declining, while that of the sick is as rapidly increasing. Dr. Miller, whose practice, as his skill, exceeds that of any other physician, is almost weary of a scene of such complicated horrors. My heart sickens at the perpetual recital to which I am compelled to be an auditor, and I long to plunge myself into woods and deserts where the faintest blast of rumor may not reach me.

Thursday morning. The die is cast. E. H. S. is dead. O the folly of prediction and the vanity of systems. In the opinion of Miller the disease in no case was ever more dreadfully and infernally malignant. He is dead. Yesterday at noon.

I am well as circumstances will permit, and shall, as soon as possible, leave the city with William Johnson for Amboy or Connecticut.

At noon on September 21, 1798, at the age of twenty-seven, Elihu Hubbard Smith breathed his last. In the *Spectator* the following notice bore testimony to the sterling worth of the young physician: "We scruple not to say that of all the victims to this fatal malady, this person will be most sincerely and universally lamented. In him science and humanity have lost one of the noblest ornaments which this age or this country has produced. To the character of a skillful and learned physician he added that of an accomplished and benevolent man. His talents were eminently diversified, and there were few departments in literature in which he had not made himself proficient."

Brown, too, had been removed to Horace Johnson's home. Although the novelist was ill, seemingly with the prevailing fever, his case responded to medicine. On Sunday the 18th he was moved to Dr. Edward Miller's residence. Three days later he wrote to Dunlap: "Most ardently do I long to shut out this city from my view, but my strength has been within these few days so totally and unaccountably subverted that I can scarcely flatter myself with being able very shortly to remove. I do not understand my own case, but see enough to discover that the combination of bodily and mental causes has made such deep inroads on the vital energies of brain and stomach, I am afraid I cannot think of departing before Monday at the least." On the 24th he wrote to his brother: "The weather has lately changed for the better, and hopes are generally entertained that the pestilence, for so it may truly be called, will decline. As to myself, I certainly improve, though slowly, and now entertain very slight apprehensions of danger to myself. Still I am anxious to leave the city. To go to Amboy and remain there for some time, will be most eligible. This calamity has endeared the survivors of the sacred fellowship, W[illiam] D[unlap], W[illiam] J[ohnson], and myself to each other in a very high degree; and I confess my wounded spirit and shattered frame will be most likely to be healed and benefited by their society. Permit me, therefore, to decline going with you to Burlington for a little while at least."

The next day, September 25, Brown addressed his brother from Perth Amboy:

It is with great pleasure that I now inform you of my safe arrival at this place. Yesterday I wrote to you informing you of my intention to come hither on the

morrow. After depositing my letter, Wm. Johnson
and myself concluded that if a water passage could
readily be found to Staten Island, it would be advisable
to depart immediately. This, being forthright sought
for, was found. We left the city at two in the afternoon, and after a most auspicious passage arrived at
Amboy at sunset. I already feel the sensations of a
new being, and am restored, as it were by magic, to a
tolerable degree of health and cheerfulness.

Here I wish to stay, at least for some weeks, in the
enjoyment of the purest air and wholesome exercise.
The change from a pestilential, desolate, and sultry
city to the odors and sprightly atmosphere of this
village is inexpressibly grateful and beneficial; and I
believe you may dismiss all uneasiness henceforth on
account of my safety.

I seize this early opportunity to inform you of my
removal, because it was due to your generous concern
for me.

Ormond; or, The Secret Witness

THE change of air," William Johnson reported from Perth Amboy on September 28, 1798, "has greatly benefited Brown and myself." Among friends of the Dunlap family and in a natural setting harmonious with Brown's eagerness to live, the young novelist cast aside gloomy thoughts as his health steadily improved and as the glow of success filled his mind with cheerful thoughts. On October 21 he departed to visit relatives in Princeton, Burlington, and Philadelphia. At home friendly comments buzzed in his ears regarding *Wieland* and the pieces in the Philadelphia *Weekly Magazine*. James Brown not only made efforts to keep the strayed Quaker in Philadelphia, but also advised him to choose subjects and characters more nearly in the ordinary current of daily experience. Hugh Maxwell, a printer, talked about issuing the completed manuscript of *Arthur Mervyn*. Zachariah Poulson, Jr., member of the Belles Lettres Society and editor of a newspaper, and other friends in prominent positions supported the family plea that Charles remain. Yet even Grandmother Armitt, now keeping more and more to her large chair by the window in anticipation of life's end, could not alter her favorite grandchild's plans.

The projected magazine, as well as the heartlifting success of *Wieland*, made Charles' return to New York City imperative. Arriving on November 15, he took up residence with the Miller brothers. Once again the members of the Friendly Club drew together with a promise to continue meeting in memory of Elihu Smith. Dunlap, hastening plans to reopen the theater, asked help in the revision of an address for the opening night. Meantime Brown wrote and issued proposals for the new monthly magazine, and he wrote steadily on several novels.

Hocquet Caritat, the publisher of *Wieland*, asked to see Brown's manuscripts. From several sets of initial chapters he chose, not *Stephen Calvert* nor *Arthur Mervyn*, but a new work, *Ormond*, about a greatminded heroine. A New Year's Day letter to Armitt contained an account of the author's daily routine and revealed the cheerful mood in which he was finishing *Ormond*:

New York, January 1, 1799

Dear Brother,

I have neither wife nor children who look up to me for food, and in spite of all refinements conjugal and paternal care can never be fully transferred to one who has neither offspring nor spouse. However this be, I will not determine. The lessons of fortitude, perhaps, are more easy to be taught than to be practiced; but this does not diminish their value. This you will admit, but will probably add that there is only vanity or folly in inculcating a lesson which the character or circumstances of the scholar disable him from learning.

As to me, the surface of my life would be thought, by most observers, tolerably smooth. I rise at eight, am seated by a comfortable fire, breakfast plenteously and in quiet and with a companion who is a model of all the social and domestic virtues. All personal and household services are performed for me without the trouble of superintendence and direction. The writing occupation is pursued with every advantageous circumstance of silence, solitude, pure air, cleanliness, and warmth.

When my voluntary and variable task is finished, I may go into the society of those from whom I derive most benefit and pleasure. That I am blind to the benefits of this condition must not be supposed. That mere external ease and temporary accommodation are sufficient to afford a reasonable being happiness must not be imagined. To forbear remembrance of the past or foresight of the future, or to confine our view to so small a part of our condition as consists in food, raiment, and repose is no argument of wisdom. These incidents have small place in the thoughts of a rational man, but I will not carry you at present beyond these or enter into all these subtilties of sensation and reflection which in spite of wealth would make me sad and in spite of poverty would make me cheerful.

It is time to end this letter. To write it was the first employment of the new year, and will be the sole employment of the kind that will take place on this day. It is an holy-day, and as such it shall be past away. Absurd enough, you will say, to make idleness a medium of amusement or an auxiliary to sanctity.

Charles Brockden Brown

On this day, all the world is busied in visiting and congratulation and feasting. I believe I shall in this instance act, in some degree, like all the world.

Adieu,

C. B. B.

Ormond; or, The Secret Witness was published some time before February 15, 1799, for on this day, in a letter to James, Brown referred to it as already printed. In its rapid preparation he had utilized the episode of the De Moivre family from "The Man at Home," the brother-sister relationship of the Beddoes in "A Series of Original Letters," and probably some incidents from *Sky-Walk*. Thus new novels were compounded partially out of fragments of less satisfactory early works. Although Brown wrote with a rapidity seemingly unparalleled in his generation, he averaged only fifteen hundred words a day. By comparison with some modern romancers this was slow progress.

Ormond is the story, as told by her friend Mrs. Sophia Westwyn Courtland, of the life of Miss Constantia Dudley, with special emphasis upon her association with the scheming Ormond. The plot is quite simple: a sixteen-year-old orphan girl gathers sufficient fortitude through years of hardship to thrust a penknife into the heart of a seducer. In a prefatory letter Brown says that his novel "will have little of that merit which flows from unity of design," because it is "a biographical sketch." The thread of narrative spirals to its conclusion; each turn introduces new characters who enter and soon disappear. There is a profusion of incidents designed to evoke emotions of pity or terror; in imitation of Anne Radcliffe's heroines this maiden is maneuvered into as many distressful circumstances as possible, not by means of seemingly supernatural incidents, but by those commonplace occurrences whereby life is rendered almost insupportable: poverty, epidemic disease, fraud, imposture, dissimulation, arrest, counterfeiting, false maxims, lack of religious faith, and threats of ravishment. The only hint of supernatural power in this novel comes in a characterization of Ormond's amazing ability to learn the thoughts and activities of people distant from him. This seeming clairvoyance results from membership in an international organization like the Illuminati. As in *Wieland* a second story parallels the main plot in Ormond's sister's strange vicissitudes which serve as a foil to those of Constantia.

Ormond is notable for its two dozen character portraits. In *Wieland* each character's "ruling passion" is a single trait carried to excess: Theodore has an excess of religious enthusiasm, Pleyel possesses an excess of rationalism, Clara wavers between these two extremes, and Carwin is a blundering mischief maker. In *Ormond* the chief characters are portrayed with greater fullness, yet essentially they are static, little changed in the end by their experiences. Several characters serve chiefly as embodiments of aspects of the ancient problem of evil or as laboratory specimens in whose degeneration may be traced the effect of crime. Although there is no brooding over diseased minds, the persons are described in terms of abnormal psychology.

Constantia Dudley is a creature of reason in whom emotions are allowed almost no play. "She reflected before she acted, and therefore acted with consistency and vigor." Excellent health makes possible a thirst for knowledge and a mind happy with thoughts of self-approbation. With no pride to subdue, she moves with dignity and courage wherever duty calls. Optimistically she prefers to die rather than beg, because her heart is usually lightened with a premonition of good fortune. Neither diffidence nor flightiness ever causes a wavering in the pursuit of goals, and "all the devils [can] not turn her out of her way." Antiquated scruples render her incapable of fraud; her virgin purity never suffers stain. In poverty and in wealth her sentiments and charitable activities remain identical; when shadows of fear or doubt cross her mind, the sunshine of self-assured rectitude promptly lights her path. Emotions of normal love are alien to her nature, and there seems to be a homosexual tendency in her conduct. She rejects all suitors, and in the end no husband awaits her.

As a rationalist Constantia fails to recognize that "sinister considerations flow in upon us through imperceptible channels and modify our thoughts in numberless ways without our being truly conscious of their presence." She is misled by her love of excellence, by her willingness to admit that Ormond and Helena are not ideally matched, and by her readiness to explore, with the possibility of altering, Ormond's theory of human nature. In this contest of wits "she was unguarded in a point where, if not her whole yet doubtless her principal, security and strongest bulwark would have existed. She was unacquainted with religion. She was unhabituated to conform herself to any standard but that connected with the present life. Matrimonial as well as every other human duty was disconnected in her mind with any awful or divine sanction. She formed her estimate of good and evil on nothing but terrestrial and visible consequences." Her plight is desperate until Sophia Westwyn, whose name symbolizes wisdom, appears as the *deus ex machina* to support with religious truth the tottering maiden. The melodramatic slaying of Ormond at the end of the tale merely enforces Brown's teaching: without the bulwark of religion no mental fortress can stand, however craftily it is supported with learning, experience, or rational estimates. Constantia lifts her hand against Ormond, not because she has recognized his deceit, but because he degenerates from a gentleman into a monster against whose attack she is forced to defend her virtue. Had Constantia overthrown the villain by reason of a newly won religious faith, she would have assumed stature as a great heroine. In this respect Martinette de Beauvais dwarfs her. As the story stands, Constantia extricates herself in the successful resolution of the plot, but the conclusion is not satisfactory. Constantia, in view of her name, deserved more strength to win her own victory, intellectually as well as physically.

The intellectually keen villain, Ormond, remains consistent to the character assigned him until the very end, when his finesse apparently gives out and he is reduced to the status of a madman. As a member of the Illuminati he desires to destroy religion, government, and family life. His secret subversive religious and political activities dictate a hostility to the institution of marriage. Flaunting a mistress, he openly de-

cries marriage as an unwise institution, and he demonstrates the force of his principle in deliberately trying
to mislead Constantia. In him evil flourishes as a result
of an intellectually conceived principle. His amazing
sources of knowledge concerning people's seemingly
hidden actions are joined with astonishing powers of
disguise (hence "The Secret Witness"). This fluent
reasoner plays fast and loose with logic with the de-
liberate intention of unsettling conventional moral
standards; his true purposes and emotions are hidden
under an almost impenetrable mask.

Sophia Westwyn, who befriends Constantia, is a
sentimentalist in the school of Lydia Languish; yet
at moments masculine aplomb and business acumen
mark her decisive actions. Endowed with wealth and
schooled in the world of fashion, she sentimentalizes
for a time over Constantia but does nothing. Suddenly
she leaves her husband in Europe, in detective fashion
hunts out Constantia, takes care of her property, tutors
her in matters of religious faith, and then leads her in
safety to Europe. Sophia's possessive nature finds satisfaction in guiding and protecting her weaker friend in
motherly fashion. "I could," she says, "but harbor
aversion to a scheme which should tend to sever me
from Constantia, or to give a competitor in her affections." The description of their reunion suggests that
Brown recognized, especially when Constantia's rejection of all suitors is recalled, an abnormal relationship: "The three succeeding days were spent in a state
of dizziness and intoxication. The ordinary functions
of nature were disturbed. The appetite for sleep and
for food were confounded and lost amidst the impet-

uosities of a master passion." Their "disclosures were of too intimate and delicate a nature." Yet, in a sense, Sophia is the embodiment of a balance between the extremes of sentimental emotional instability and "the cold dictates of discretion"; she approximates Brown's ideal woman.

Helena Cleves, Ormond's mistress, represents a woman guided only by the emotions. After Ormond penetrates her weak defense, she tries in his presence to retain cheerful spirits, but a morbid sensibility forbids indifference to the scorn of the world. Intellectual interests are lacking; her delight in music and painting symbolizes her instability. She flutters to every breeze vibrating her heart strings; she knows no security when her lover casts her off. "Her education has disabled her from standing alone." Her suicide arises from an inability to cope with this world when black despair replaces the optimism of her misguided love.

Martinette de Beauvais represents the self-reliant, masculine-minded woman; wide travel and strange experiences have fashioned her into a poker-faced deceiver playing for high stakes in the game of national politics. At fourteen she resisted the advances of a base priest. At eighteen she studied politics and married Wentworth, "a political enthusiast who esteemed nothing more graceful or glorious than to die for the liberties of mankind." "A wild spirit of adventure and a boundless devotion" to her husband led her to cross the ocean in 1778 to assist in the American Revolution. Often she saved Wentworth by killing his adversary. In 1789 as one of the subverters of monarchy in France, she fought in the ranks so dauntlessly that her "hand never faltered when liberty demanded the victim." Delegated to simulate the part of a banished royalist, she thus gained access to and assassinated the Duke of Brunswick. In the yellow fever epidemic in Philadelphia in 1793 she unhesitatingly digs a grave for her guardian and at night drags his body there for burial. Fearless and sagacious, Martinette yet plays consoling airs on a lute and speaks softly in many languages. She combines the callous strength of masculinity with the soft grace of femininity.

Lady D'Arcy, a benefactress of Martinette, vacillates in religion, marriage, and love because "she [is] open to every new impression. She [is] the dupe of every powerful reasoner, and assume[s] with equal facility the most opposite shapes." Her character reveals the pitfalls menacing the person who has no firmly established guiding maxims.

Craig has the criminal type of mind. Birth under an unfavorable star destined him to a life of theft and dishonesty. The law of his nature drives him to extremes of malignity in every act and in every deed, as in his gift of counterfeit bills to Constantia in the darkest hour of her need. This typical villain, who lies about his family and refuses to support his mother, represents undisguised, crude, unintellectual, and ungifted dishonesty. Martynne, who appears only briefly at the end, is of a different stripe. With his dishonesty goes a quality of dissimulation not found in Craig. His wickedness is not so much that of a malignant spirit as that of dishonest pretension.

Stephen Dudley, Constantia's father, is one of the most interesting characters in the novel; he typifies all that practical America disliked in the artistic temperament. Educated as a painter in Europe, he returns unwillingly to New York to conduct an apothecary shop inherited from his father. Spiraling wealth increases his melancholy as he contemplates his humiliating and ignominious position, which renders impossible further activity in those "pursuits which exalt and harmonize the feelings." Craig on taking over supervision of the store systematically embezzles funds. At the end of two years this dishonesty is discovered too late; every shred of the property is lost. Dudley moves to Philadelphia where painting does not afford a livelihood, and where music teaching is treated with general contempt. His native melancholy is increased by blindness arising from a cataract. Having taken to drink, he suffers every shade of deprivation until Ormond assumes the obligation to repay Craig's thefts and Helena wills her property to Constantia. Again in affluence, Dudley recovers his cheerfulness of spirit and undergoes a successful operation for the restoration of his sight. Brown's comment is interesting: "Perhaps, in a rational estimate, one of the most fortunate events that could have befallen those persons was that period of adversity through which they had been doomed to pass. Most of the defects that adhered to the character of Mr. Dudley had, by this means, been exterminated." Sweet are the uses of adversity: artists must experience hardship to bring them to their senses!

In *Ormond* each character is a personification of an abstract quality, virtue or vice, and the actions of each person constitute a lesson in conduct. The choice of names for Sophia and Constantia is not the sole clue to this interpretation; the characters illustrate the injunction that it is better to teach by example than rule. Baxter's death as a result of unreasoning fear serves to introduce this comment: "His case may be quoted as an example of the force of imagination." Brown the moralist again exemplifies in a novel some important truths regarding the moral constitution of man.

The story teaches the perviousness of disaster or fraud to those who are unschooled in the whole art of self-defense. Constantia Dudley manages through superior power of reasoning to fend for her father and herself in routine household and personal matters, but when a dishonest man skilled in deceit assails her with all the arts of cunning, she is unable to perceive his dishonesty because she lacks the bulwark of religious faith. Brown here poses an important problem: What is the place of religion in personal life? If *Wieland* teaches that too much religion may lead to mania, then *Ormond* arrives at the conclusion that religious faith is absolutely indispensable in the attainment of a happy life. Fear, terror, imposture, forgery, deceit, criminal-mindedness, and dishonesty can overthrow men and women whose education has been sensuous or rational; the surest defense against any pitfall is a firm religious faith.

In Brown's series of novels notable for aphoristic power, *Ormond* is superior in its commentary upon the major political, economic, religious, and personal problems. Some of the maxims in this book are:

The strongest mind is swayed by circumstances. There is no firmness of integrity, perhaps, able to repel every species of temptation which is produced by the present constitution of human affairs; and yet temptation is successful chiefly by virtue of its gradual and invisible approaches.

Happiness is only attendant on the performance of duty.

Human life abounds with mysterious appearances.

Homely liberty is better than splendid servitude.

The company of one with whom we have no sympathy nor sentiments in common is, of all species of solitude, the most loathsome and dreary.

Marriage is an instrument of pleasure or pain in proportion as equality is more or less.

In no case, perhaps, is the decision of a human being impartial or totally uninfluenced by sinister and unselfish motives.

The many nuggets of wisdom do not compensate for technical weakness in narration. Although all the episodes have relevance to the theme of the novel, they are introduced with insufficient skill. Were all the scenes fully delineated, were there conversations and descriptions to give dramatic surge to the events, and were the proportion better between Constantia's early life and the brief passage with Ormond, the novel would be stronger. But Brown was desirous of giving his readers instruction rather than entertainment; he labored over the maxims and dashed through years of action in a paragraph. His language, as always, is Latinized. Occasionally he slips, as when he has Craig's body lying "supine" although "his face rested on the floor." Pronoun reference is often faulty, and the characters are named long after they are introduced. Late in the tale a parenthesis is used to announce

the information that the Dudleys had assumed the
name of Acworth upon moving from New York to
Philadelphia. Sophia's discovery of Constantia is the
more miraculous in the light of this circumstance.
Dudley's wife dies on one page, and five pages later
she is an object of peevish reproaches.

Yet *Ormond* has the virtue of dealing with the immediate social problems of poverty, of survival in the
midst of plague, of maintaining integrity in the presence of deceit, of unmasking conspirators linked with
international subversive organizations, and of achieving a satisfactory pattern of life for attaining happiness.
Although there is almost no local color, no precise
description of characters or places, there are a few
excellent pictures of the plague, some deft characteriza-
tions, and a hair-raising climax.

The structure of *Ormond* is in broad outline like
that of Godwin's *Caleb Williams* wherein one main
character is treated in detail before a second enters
the story at about the half-way mark. The senten-
tious style also is reminiscent of Godwin. But the
leading characters, the emphasis upon sex, and the
melodramatic ending derive from Anne Radcliffe's
Gothic novels, such as *The Mysteries of Udolpho*
wherein Emily St. Aubert goes unharmed through
three volumes of narrow escapes. Emily and Constantia are cast in the same mold. Both are victims of
circumstances; both are in poverty. Both are betrayed
by seeming benefactors. Both are creatures of reason
and do not yield to their emotions. Both are educated
by their fathers in the classics. Both are sweet and
brave with the souls of fortitude. No obstacle or

sorrow is sufficiently great to daunt them. Both prefer death to a stained reputation. In *Ormond* the emphasis on sex occurs not merely through the several scenes of seduction, but it is pervasive throughout the analysis of the fundamental psychology of the characters. No other early American writer of fiction has so consistently examined his characters in terms of their sexual responses.

Favorable public reaction to *Ormond* was immediate. On July 4, 1799, Samuel Harrison Smith, editor of *Universal Gazette*, published a long review of the novel and an appraisal of the ability of the author:

In the United States we are deeply interested in exciting and cherishing a talent for this species of composition. Its happiest and perhaps its most important exercise consists in the accurate delineation of existing manners. In this case it ridicules follies which ought to be avoided; it lashes vices which ought to be abhorred. It compares what is with that which ought to be, and strives to supplant existing evil by attainable good. At present we almost wholly depend upon Europe for productions of this character. Whatever intrinsic merit they may possess, this merit loses much if not the whole of its force when the work that exhibits it crosses the Atlantic. The manners of Europe differ essentially from those of this country. Characters there drawn are not here understood, and morals there of infinite consequence here are of little moment.

From these considerations, it results that this species of writing ought to be native. Every effort therefore made to improve it merits encomium. We hesitate not, then, to return the author of *Ormond* our unqualified thanks. His motives entitle him to esteem. . . .

In 1802 *Ormond* was translated into German by Friedrich Oertel and published in Leipzig by Beygang. Years later Percy Bysshe Shelley became enamored of the book and its rationalistic heroine. Yet in spite of its highly interesting nature, *Ormond* remains the least popularly esteemed of Brown's four important novels.

·12·

Arthur Mervyn;
or, Memoirs of the Year 1793

THE successful publication of *Wieland* and *Ormond* gave Brown the necessary self-confidence to complete projects which earlier had been dropped. Publishers were vying for his manuscripts. The new cultural patriotism was leading a few venturesome printers and booksellers to formulate plans for an American publishing industry equal to that of England. Caritat, the bookseller, was steadily expanding his publishing activities. Printers like Maxwell in Philadelphia and Hopkins in New York were looking for new manuscripts. The financial risk of publishers was great; scattered population areas created difficult sales problems. Yet the reception of *Wieland* and *Ormond* encouraged enterprising publishers to see in native works a promise of profit.

Trade practices in the distribution of books through

booksellers were not quite the same as those of other industries. Job-lot selling to a middleman was seldom employed, so that the appearance of a work on the shelves of booksellers in widely scattered communities depended largely upon chance. A few cities—Boston, New York, Philadelphia, and Baltimore—developed local area markets, but the cost of transportation and inadequate credit facilities made long-distance book distribution prohibitive. The national distribution of books in large quantities was still to be devised. Not until 1802 did Mathew Carey attempt to create a smoothly functioning wholesale market through the formation of the American Company of Booksellers. In these circumstances an American author in the 1790's had to depend almost entirely for income on sales within the trading area in which his books were printed. In competition with his book were all British publications. Nearly every ship captain bought a few boxes of books and disposed of them at American ports, so that the seaboard cities had a constant inflow of new books. The number constituted only a trickle by comparison with the great stream possible. Yet the amount was adequate to provide inventories for stores and thus to dull the enthusiasm of bankers asked to back new American ventures. Brown's merchant brothers warned again and again that the market was insufficient to support native authors. Undeterred by this common-sense businessman's view of wasted effort, the novelist refused to remain in Philadelphia or to forsake a vocation which within a half year had elevated him from obscurity into fame.

On the completion of *Ormond,* Brown turned to

the story of Arthur Mervyn, the first chapters of which had been published in the Philadelphia *Weekly Magazine*. This novel, *Arthur Mervyn; or, Memoirs of the Year 1793*, relates the experiences of a curiosity-driven eighteen-year-old country lad, who, during the yellow fever epidemic of 1793 in Philadelphia, stumbles upon almost every species of dishonesty. He is the employee of Thomas Welbeck, a forger, murderer, and seducer who effectively applies a sophistical wisdom and diabolical skill to his nefarious schemes. Yet the humanitarian, honest, investigative, marriage-minded lad is never misled into committing evil acts or abandoning his high purposes. This novel recounts an exciting, yet moralizing, tale in which great criminality is opposed by disinterested honesty.

The pattern derives from German tales of banditry like Tschokke's *Abœllino, The Great Bandit*. As practiced in Europe, banditry was comparatively unknown in the United States. To employ an American setting satisfactorily while using a popular oversea story model, Brown turned his villain into an imposter, embezzler, forger, and defaulter. These qualities were most feared by businessmen in a time when personal probity was relied upon in the fulfillment of contracts. The youthful hero triumphantly demonstrates that a life of integrity and of devotion to the welfare of others alone brings happiness.

The two parts of *Arthur Mervyn* form a work much like Godwin's *Caleb Williams* not only because the two heroes possess a similar curiosity, but also because the varied subject matter illustrates a single idea. The incidents are uniformly within the range of ordinary experience. Of Brown's four important novels, *Arthur Mervyn* comes closest to making a transcript of real life. The background—the devastating yellow fever epidemic of 1793—was fresh in the minds of most people in the Philadelphia area. The scenes of 1798 had not been so terrifying or gruesome, but the fear brought to mind vivid recollections of death symbols chalked on row after row of houses, of the frantic enmity to impromptu hospitals, of mass emigrations to rural homes, of hysteria causing suicide, of death by the thousands, of the tinkling bell announcing the death cart, and of the pillage of the deserted city by thieves.

It will be recalled that Brown had been visiting Smith in Wethersfield, Connecticut, in the late summer of 1793, so that the novelist reported at second-hand the scenes which he described so vividly. Yet during the New York epidemic of 1798, the novelist came down with the fever, and felt the chill horror of events both as a patient and as a nurse. The incident of Dr. Scandella's introducing the disease into his rooming house served as the basis for a dramatic scene in the novel.

But the plague forms only one of several strands in the narrative. The story is primarily that of an ardent youth seeking to make his way honestly in a corrupt world. Curiosity brings a prompt introduction to evil in many forms and to the baseness of some people's standards of value and morality. He learns of one partner's scheming to defraud another. He comes upon the still-smoking pistol of a murderer, and he helps to bury the victim. He seeks to aid a betrayed and helpless foreign girl, and he bursts into a house of prostitution with a reformer's zeal. He sees that vengeance rather than justice operates when good men are forced to rot in debtor's prison. He feels the scorpion sting of slanderous gossip. Fraud and guile, deceit and dissimulation, as hazards in everyday life, supply a second strand in the novel.

Abstract moralizing appears less often in this novel than in the earlier ones, for Brown is concerned with practical action in a world of sin and suffering. Yet Arthur's deeds and words comprise a third strand, the white of blameless character intertwining with the red and black of murder and dishonesty. Through his mind surge undefined aspirations to improve society; he tries to regenerate criminals, to prevent dishonesty, to dull the edge of sorrow, to comfort the stricken, to temper vengeance with mercy, and to bring happiness to all. Although not so obviously a moralized tale as *Ormond*, the story of Arthur Mervyn seeks similarly to teach lessons through the hero's exemplary conduct.

Brown published *Arthur Mervyn* in two parts and through two publishers. The first part was issued by Maxwell in Philadelphia before May 21, 1799; the second part was printed by George F. Hopkins in New York before July 4, 1800.

Part I of *Arthur Mervyn* is an exciting, self-contained unit beginning and ending with the hero's leaning against a wall in Philadelphia. A farmer's son, Arthur comes to Philadelphia from Chester County because his widowed father has married a milkmaid of unsavory reputation. Arthur finds an abandoned baby, meets the forger Welbeck and a boy and girl whom the schemer defrauded, sees Welbeck holding a smoking pistol after murdering Captain Watson, comes upon a frenzied girl planning suicide, and seeks to mitigate the horrors of the plague by becoming superintendent of a hospital.

In Part II Arthur is rescued from almost certain death by Dr. Stevens, the narrator, and later from arrest because of accusations of willing partnership in Welbeck's crimes. The youth falls in and out of love with Eliza Hadwin, rescues Miss Achsa Fielding from a house of prostitution where the mistress shoots him for intruding, visits a prison to console and reclaim the dying Welbeck, and goes to Baltimore to return Watson's money which Welbeck has surrendered. Arthur settles down with Dr. Stevens to study medicine and to enjoy normal social contacts. Miss Fielding in relating the involved story of her life reveals the extent of her fortune. Arthur proposes, and the finale of the story is the revelation that Miss Fielding is a Jewess.

Like most sequels, this one fails to maintain the same high pitch of excitement as the first part. Part I pictures Arthur in the grip of circumstances likely to topple him to ruin; he seems guided by a perverse fate slowly throttling his life. Part II, however, makes Arthur the chief actor who triumphs over obstacles and who rescues erring and abused people. The mood shifts from terror at the dangers into which the hero walks to indignation at the vices he tilts against or to pathos at the victims of crime or delusion. These emotions, which are capable of sustaining long fiction, are likely to be, as they are here, rendered ineffective when preceded by events striking upon nerves taut with fear. This novel teaches practical lessons. The moralist continues to phrase bits of abstract wisdom. "It is every one's duty," he says, "to profit by all opportunities of inculcating the lessons of justice and humanity." In respect to the epidemic, wisdom consists in maintaining calmness and avoiding unnecessary fear. Brown does not censure flight to the country, but he counsels persons of humane spirit to remain as organizers of health services or as nurses in hospitals and stricken homes. Adequate supplies of water, he suggests, can wash away the accumulations of filth piled outside houses. Cleanliness is of more value in eliminating disease than the sprinkling of vinegar, the burning of tar, the ringing of bells, or the shooting of gunpowder—the four common remedies popularly applied. Convinced that a layman can do good, the novelist gives common-sense advice in its most palatable form.

Marital irregularity and immoral conduct exemplify the evils flowing from association with persons of vicious propensities, as in Sawny Mervyn's unhappy end, Wallace's infidelity, and Welbeck's ruinous relationship with Mrs. Villars. Other themes include vengeful imprisonment for debt, the humane use of wealth, and the rehabilitation of criminals.

The number of maxims in *Arthur Mervyn* is small. Yet the following show no diminution in power or alteration in point of view:

Sincerity is always safest.
Life is a trivial sacrifice in the cause of duty.

The past is without remedy; but the future is, in some degree, within our power to create and fashion.

Honest purposes, though they may not bestow happiness on others, will at least secure it to him who fosters them.

If cities are the chosen seats of misery and vice, they are likewise the soil of all the laudable and strenuous production of mind.

Indignation at wrong is the truest test of virtue.

The standard of possibilities, especially in vice and virtue, is fashioned by most men after their own character.

•I3•

Edgar Huntly;
or, Memoirs of a Sleep-Walker

I FIND to be the writer of *Wieland* and *Ormond* is a greater recommendation than I ever imagined it would be," wrote Brown to his brother James. Fame had rapped on the young novelist's door. And strangers came rapping, too. Travelers from abroad were taken to him, just as they were ushered into the presence of Alexander Hamilton and other dignitaries in New York City. Brown and Johnson retained the rooms at 45 Pine Street; here came, among other visitors, the British novelist John Davis who was gathering material for a book of travels: "I sought acquaintance with a man who had acquired so much intellectual renown. I found Mr. Brown quite in the costume of an author, embodying virtue in a new novel, and making his pen fly before him." "A great coat and shoes down at heel" betrayed America's inadequate support of her artists. Davis continued: "Mr. Brown occupied a dismal room in a dismal street. I asked whether a view of nature would not be more propitious to composition, or whether he should not write with more facility were his window to command the prospect of the Lake of Geneva. 'Sir,' he said, 'good pens, thick paper, and ink well diluted would facilitate my composition more than the prospect of the broadest expanse of water or mountains rising above the clouds.' "

This comment to Davis is the more revealing, when it is recalled that at this very time, April, 1799, Brown was seeing *Arthur Mervyn* through the press, was engaged in writing *Edgar Huntly*, and was sending to press the first issue of the *Monthly Magazine*, of which he was editor. Little inspiration came from outward nature, although there always recurred the dream of finding health, that first wealth, in occasional journeys.

In June, Brown joined William Johnson on a tour of Connecticut to visit friends made with Elihu on their jaunts in 1793 and 1797. At Middletown they were guests of Richard Alsop, the poet and merchant, whose stay in New York had endeared him to the Friendly Club. Alsop planned excursions along the river and to the striking trap rock formations on the nearby hills. The novelist jotted in his diary a number of remarks which indicate heightened exhilaration and improved health. Especially did he plan to preserve "the impressions which this journey shall make, in a way that may serve a public and a private purpose. Connecticut has never been described, and surely merits a description."

Travel books were becoming increasingly popular. Dozens of Europeans after a few months' stay in the United States were publishing distorted, ill-formed, jibing commentaries upon American scenery and manners. To these distasteful descriptions was being added an ever increasing amount of native humor having as its butt of ridicule the character of the New England or Yankee people. The wooden nutmeg had already given Connecticut its nickname, although the natives thought of themselves as dwellers in "the land of steady habits." It was indeed time that someone accept responsibility for preparing accurate topographical and cultural surveys of the American scene with a view of ending the petty bickering separating states and regions.

"I had a vigilant eye," Brown wrote, "for passing objects, roads, dwellings, and passengers. My curiosity was awakened by the intention I had formed of describing what I saw. In this respect my mind has undergone a sudden and memorable revolution. Instead of being, as I used to be, sluggish, torpid, and inattentive, my eye is watchful and my mind busy in arranging and comparing objects." This good intention unhappily went for naught. Descriptive skill nowhere appeared to replace the usual vague generalization. "On Saturday we reached Middletown," he continued. "It was evening, and a bright sky, a smooth road, and healthful state of my frame allowed me to take in all the pleasure which the circumstances of the time and place were calculated to afford. Never did I receive equal delight from a rural prospect. Yet how much a matter of association and moral sensibility is the sensation flowing from the survey of the grandeur of nature." Again there was a rapid transition from the external to the internal world, from the objective to the subjective point of view. Sustained word photography was not within the capacity of the moralizing essayist: "Had I not had some previous acquaintance with this scene, through the medium of actual observation and books, my sensations would have been widely different and much less lively and exuberant. Had I not anticipated intercourse with those whose society is dear to me, my feelings would have been comparatively mean and insignificant."

Every trifling incident, he thought, "would serve to illustrate manners and gratify the curiosity," since "there is a method of narration which would make interesting the most common and familiar theme." How far this novelist with three books to his credit failed to achieve a successful descriptive-narrative account may be seen in the following passage:

Mrs. J., her sister, and Miss —— were the females. D., A[lsop], Johnson, and myself accompanied them. The fear of bad roads, reptiles, and water mars the pleasure of many excursions like this. I never met with women so totally exempt from these terrors as were our companions. The river was twice crossed, once after night and in a blustering atmosphere, in a crazy boat crowded with carriages and horses. The road was in some parts precipitous and dangerous, and was traversed during our return in the dark. I was a stranger to the way, had bad eyes, and drove with precipitation; yet Miss ——, my companion in a chaise, betrayed not the slightest apprehension and concern. We ascended a hill which, from the abundance of its rattlesnakes, is known by the name of rattlesnake hill;

we clambered over rocks and pits, but the name of snake seemed to affect the females as little as that of butterfly.

After recounting further visits to beauty spots along the Connecticut River, such as Job's Pool and the nearby mountains, Brown concluded this account with characteristic reflections: "This day was full of incidents, and productive of much fatigue; yet I remember it with powerful and pleasant emotion. To what cause is this to be ascribed? Does it flow from its social circumstances? What a wretched possession is solitude. Intelligence and sympathy beaming from eye to eye constitute all the happiness of man. Nature owes all her charms to her alliance with images flowing from society." Such a report seems inadequate from the pen of the novelist who was engaged in writing *Edgar Huntly*, the first American novel to portray wilderness scenes for the purpose of exciting wonder. Yet true to his character, Brown was always a moralist examining life for its meaning to humanity. He extracted generalizations from experience as a bee sucks nectar from a flower.

On July 26, 1799, Brown felt the general dejection and inquietude marking the annual return of the plague to New York. The excessive heat induced exhaustion, and his spirits and mental vigor declined. This year he would not remain: "My sensations in this state of things are so different from my sensations last summer that I look back with astonishment. I do not wonder that I then remained in the city, but that my mind retained its tranquility in the midst of perils the most imminent, that I could muse and write cheerfully in spite of the groans of the dying and the rumbling of hearses, and in spite of a thousand tokens of indisposition in my own frame, is now almost incredible. I perceive that this tranquility and courage is utterly beyond my reach at present." Tentatively he and Johnson planned to sail up the Hudson to Albany and to visit Niagara Falls during the dangerous weeks in August and September.

Brown published a sample of *Edgar Huntly; or, Memoirs of a Sleep-Walker* in the first issue of his magazine, *The Monthly Magazine and American Review* of April, 1799. On July 26 he wrote to James as if the completed manuscript had been delivered to Hugh Maxwell, the Philadelphia printer and publisher. Late in the summer, copies were placed on sale. Immediately the novel gained popularity and a second edition was published on February 13, 1801.

In *Edgar Huntly* Brown dropped the portrayal of sophistical villains like Ormond and Welbeck to return to the psychological probing of *Wieland.* Again the actions of men and women suffering from delusions and manias evoke terror, but wilderness scenery, Indian hostility, and sleepwalking add an original quality. The novel concerns a lad, Edgar Huntly, who seeks the murderer of his friend Waldegrave. At first suspicion points to Clithero Edny, but in the end it is revealed that an Indian was responsible. The narrative ostensibly is a long letter written in great excitement by Huntly to his sweetheart, Mary Waldegrave, to enforce the lesson that good intentions when not guided by reason often lead to harmful results. "I have erred," says Huntly, "not through sinister or malignant intentions, but from the impulse of misguided, indeed, but powerful benevolence."

Edgar Huntly is a superb American version of the eighteenth-century Gothic novel. The setting is in the "western wilderness" among the rugged mountain steeps of the Upper Delaware River Valley, where ravines and waterfalls are numerous, where gray cougars skulk among caves, and where Indians make incursions upon settlements. Here are the three romantic themes of the American frontier used for the first time: rugged scenery, wild animals, and savage redskins. Although James Fenimore Cooper, in the original preface to *The Spy*, sneered at Brown's cave scene containing "an American, a savage, a wild cat, and a tomahawk, in a conjunction that never did, nor ever will occur," several scenes in the Leatherstocking Tales are reminiscent of and indeed less plausible than this one. The success of *Edgar Huntly* helped fix the setting of many American novels in the wilderness and lent impetus to the movement for picturing native scenery and native characters. The Indians are wooden types serving merely to arouse horror. Queen Mab, a wizened old crone, is a new character in American fiction; Scott's portrayal of a similar old woman led a later critic to complain that no novel is complete without such a person.

A Gothic novel seeks above all else to arouse emotions of terror. As an American with nationalistic feelings, Brown discards the well-worn devices of Mrs. Anne Radcliffe, "puerile superstition and exploded manners, Gothic castles and chimeras," in favor of "the incidents of Indian hostility, and the perils of the western wilderness." This terrain differs little in ruggedness or local color from Mrs. Radcliffe's Alpine scenes; the upper reaches of the Delaware River appear as a desert, with shrub oaks and dwarf cedars as emblems of its sterile and uncultivated state. In the rugged, mountainous, picturesque, and wild countryside there actually are deep thickets, precipices, limestone caverns, ravines, and turbulent streams.

This background is perfectly suitable for ghastly events, because savage redskins and wild animals roam in these mountain fastnesses. Indian cruelty had been a theme of complaint for almost two centuries; lurking on the fringes of civilization, these painted savages silently penetrate homes and strike innocent victims. Brown makes no effort to picture the Indians in their camps or villages or to enter into their psychology; he simply reports their presence as if their normal activity were one of bloodshed. Huntly's deranged mind builds up a benevolent conception of these people, but in action the lad assumes, as did many other white men, that the only good Indian is a dead Indian. Huntly's parents had died in a raid. When he meets a redskin guarding the entrance to a cave, he asks no questions; he kills him. At no time are the Indians given an opportunity to speak for themselves; their hostility is taken for granted, and at the earliest opportunity every red man is shot to death.

Blood flows freely in this novel. The Indians run true to form in mangling maidens as well as men. Huntly's love of living things makes him unwilling to take the life of an animal, but in cold blood he unhesitatingly shoots five unarmed Indians. To one of these he gives a gory quietus by a bayonet thrust. At the very end of the story Clithero appears blood-stained after an encounter with a new set of Indians. The gruesome details are never dwelt upon; yet Brown introduces to later fictionists the principle that blood-shed and scalping are essential in frontier fiction.

The action of the novel takes place largely at night, since "intense dark is the parent of fears." Huntly's first excursions occur after sunset, because "a nocturnal journey in districts so romantic and wild as these . . . is more congenial to my temper than a noonday ramble." He first sees Clithero digging under the elm at night, and on three succeeding nights he plays sleuth. As the moon declines, the gloom increases, and the country-side assumes an unfriendly attitude. Emotions become greatly exaggerated in darkness; tense nerves respond to slight sounds. Fear rises with every new experience.

The darkness of night is made more terrifying by the darkness of caves, wherein several important inci-dents occur. Exceptionally interesting is an episode of Huntly's awakening in a pit. Although Brown's gener-alized description usually is inadequate, the very nature of this scene gives excellence to his method. Huntly awakes in a cold, dark place rather than in the bed to which he had retired. His body aches from seemingly repeated blows from a club, his temples throb, and a cold sweat dampens his face. He fears he is blind. His mind rapidly tests every plausible interpretation of his strange plight. He feels around with hands and feet; he realizes that he is in a vast and irregular earthen apartment; he kicks a tomahawk. Pain and terror induce a species of delirium. Hunger and thirst assail him. He hears an unequal and varying echo, sometimes dying away and sometimes swelling into loudness. The wailing cry of a panther is peculiarly terrifying. Two lights glow—the eyes of the panther. A crashing stroke with the tomahawk fells the animal, struggling and shrieking. From the mouth of the cave he sees four Indians lying beside a fire, and he hears the groans of a captive maiden, whom he rescues.

Huntly's pains are not identified, his emotions are not analyzed precisely, and his actions are not reported dramatically; yet this generalized narrative, because it leaves the reader with a sense of terror at the hero's plight, maintains an agonized suspense. An eerie strangeness emerges in these suspense scenes. Just after a dreadful event has occurred, the character meditates upon all sides of the matter and indulges in a good deal of self-commiseration at his unparalleled fate. The psychologizing at these moments serves to heighten the excitement by clarifying the insanity of the chief actors. At times Brown hints that a terrible event is to take place, but each character, before acting, thinks through all possible eventualities. Clithero at the door of Mrs. Lorimer, when he meditates murder, says, "Is it right to proceed? Can I bear the spectacle of wounds and of blood? What can I do? Cannot my guilt be extenuated? Is there not a good I can do?" Similarly, Huntly never proceeds without interrogating his motives.

The events cover a very short span of time and follow with great rapidity. As in all good terror fiction the unexpected occurs frequently. Just as Clithero is about to strike the sleeping Clarissa, Mrs. Lorimer shrieks and diverts the blow. Clithero had unwittingly aimed at his sweetheart, who is saved by the intended victim.

Yet Brown does not get effects by violating the canons of fictional motivation. Every incident is carefully prepared in advance. The elm tree by which the murder of Waldegrave occurs is pointed out with as much volubility as if a guide were addressing tourists. Huntly's first visit to the cave and the description of the contiguous territory prepare for the pit scene. His strange antics foreshadow insanity and sleepwalking. There are several explanations for Huntly's appearance in the pit, special prominence being given to details which indicate that Huntly fell while sleepwalking. It is a tribute to Brown's skill that most readers, despite these clues and the title of the novel, discover with astonishment the actual cause. This trick of multiple explanation of an incident reappears in Hawthorne's tales and novels.

The psychological probing gives depth to the characterization of Clithero and Huntly. Clithero Edny thinks that his life is dominated by supernatural power. An "unconscious necessity" had led to his shooting of Wiatte in Ireland. "Smitten with an excess of thought" and disturbed by Mrs. Lorimer's obstinate persuasion that her fate was linked with Wiatte's, Clithero develops the morbid notion that he has rescued his life at the expense of hers; his "fancy begins to be infected with the errors of his understanding." He suffers from delusions of guilt, and in exculpating his attempt to murder Mrs. Lorimer, he declares that he is under the compulsive guidance of a supernatural power. As Sarsefield realizes, Clithero has become hopelessly insane. The sleepwalking is tangible evidence of unbalanced mentality.

In developing this story by using parallel characters, Brown takes the youthful Edgar Huntly along a path similar to Clithero's. In the beginning Huntly is "principally stimulated by an ungovernable curiosity." A vague desire to avenge Waldegrave's death is soon altered to an obsession that he is commissioned to be of service to mankind and to restore Clithero from derangement to reason. Curiosity like that of Caleb Williams and Arthur Mervyn drives him to uncover Clithero's box and to read Mrs. Lorimer's memoirs. Now knowing Clithero's innocence, Huntly pursues him to the ravine, where a panther is seen falling to death in an unsuccessful leap across the chasm. At home again, Huntly dreams that Waldegrave's form flits before him as a reminder of a duty remaining to be performed, "which I had culpably neglected." The dementia here is identical with that of the two Wielands. A reading of Waldegrave's letters induces "a degree of wavering and dejection." Huntly obviously has now passed over the shadowy line into delusion. From this symptom to sleepwalking is but a short step. The revelation is made skillfully: Inglefield tells of the walking in the garret; Sarsefield reports seeing a lad dressed like Huntly in a trancelike walk at night; and finally Huntly recounts his sensations upon recovering consciousness in the pit. Huntly's terrifying exploits in the cave and with the Indians bear no relation to his insanity, but immediately upon his return to

Inglefield's he insists upon trying to cure Clithero's madness. Huntly's misguided efforts lead to tragic sorrow for the Sarsefields, because Mrs. Sarsefield opens a letter whose terrifying contents induce the premature birth of a child which dies. Brown leaves in mid-air the matter of the cure of Huntly's obsession; with the disappearance of its cause, it presumably vanishes.

The strange superstition at the basis of Clithero's insanity had been used earlier by Brown, but nowhere else does he dwell with equal emphasis upon the terrifying results of believing that a mysterious tie exists between two people, so that the death of one inevitably causes the death of another. Mrs. Lorimer and Wiatte are twins; doubtless the superstition arose from the strange similarity of the fates of identical twins. Yet Brown, in a curiously parallel incident, introduces Weymouth as a friend of Waldegrave. "I loved Waldegrave," says Weymouth, "and know not any person in the world whose life was dearer to me than his. . . . With his life, my own existence and property were, I have reason to think, inseparably united." Brown never concludes this subject, but it is an interesting device by which he seeks to enforce a momentary belief in the existence of mystic connections between human beings. Poe develops this idea in his most famous story, "The Fall of the House of Usher," wherein Roderick Usher dies at the same moment as his twin sister.

A few quotations will illustrate the psychological data included in *Edgar Huntly;* the modernity of some of the conclusions gives evidence of Brown's penetrating insight into this new field of learning.

The incapacity of sound sleep denotes a mind sorely wounded. It is thus that atrocious criminals denote the possession of some dreadful secret.

A considerable portion of time and amplification of phrase are necessary to exhibit, verbally, ideas contemplated in a space of incalculable brevity.

Frenzy, like prejudice, is curable.

Intense dark is always the parent of fears.

Every man, not himself the victim of irretrievable disasters, perceives the folly of ruminating on the past, and of fostering a grief which cannot reverse or recall the decrees of an immutable necessity; but every man who suffers is unavoidably shackled by the errors which he censures in his neighbor, and his efforts to relieve himself are as fruitless as those with which he attempted the relief of others.

Most men are haunted by some species of terror or antipathy, which they are for the most part able to trace to some incident which befell them in their early years.

Maxims on social topics also appear as evidence of the command Brown had over his materials. The excellence of apothegms, as Dr. Samuel Johnson observes, "consists not so much in the expression of some rare or abstruse sentiment, as in the comprehension of some useful truth in few words."

Curiosity like virtue is its own reward. Knowledge is of value for its own sake, and pleasure is annexed to the acquisition without regard to anything beyond. It is precious even when disconnected with moral inducements and heartfelt sympathies.

Remorse is an ample and proper expiation for all offenses. . . . It is only the obdurate and exulting criminal that is worthy of our indignation. It is common for pity to succeed the bitterest suggestions of resentment.

The vices of servitude are less hateful than those of tyranny.

Death is but a shifting of the scene; and the endless progress of eternity, which to the good is merely the perfection of felicity, is to the wicked an accumulation of woe. The self-destroyer is his own enemy.

Affluence and dignity, however valuable, may be purchased too dear. Honesty will not take away its keenness from the winter blast, its ignominy and unwholesomeness from servile labor, or strip of its charms the life of elegance and leisure; but these, unaccompanied with self-reproach, are less deplorable than wealth and honor, the possession of which is marred by our own disapprobation.

No one knows the powers that are latent in his constitution. Called forth by imminent dangers, our efforts frequently exceed our most sanguine belief.

Separately paged at the end of the third volume of *Edgar Huntly,* and added to expand the volume to book length, is "Death of Cicero, A Fragment," a short story about Brown's favorite Roman author. It is a letter to Atticus from Tiro, a devoted follower, who attempts to conduct the proscribed orator to safety in a foreign land. His efforts fail because a storm renders a voyage impossible and because Cicero refuses to hide from danger. The aged orator says that he has run his course of life and that he is ready to die. Antony's posse comes. With one blow Cicero's head is severed. In this story Brown reconstructs an actual historical event, but again the method is expository rather than narrative. As in *Edgar Huntly,* emphasis rests on man's authorship of his own unhappy destiny. This story also foreshadows Brown's growing interest in politics, a result in part of his fear that the United States might be subverted by alien doctrines or false leadership.

After writing four excellent novels and numerous fragments, all in the tradition of the terror novel as modified by a concern with ideas, Brown let himself be maneuvered into editorial and hack work. Fame had rapped at his door, but he found honor without a golden accompaniment quite useless. His merchant brothers were faring better. He, too, would guard the main chance.

The Monthly Magazine & American Review

SMITH'S suggestion that the Friendly Club sponsor a magazine had been warmly received in the spring of 1798. His death had the effect of spurring his friends to extraordinary activity. "Elihu would have us do this," these young men said to each other, and straightway they went about completing plans. Brown became convinced that a monthly magazine, with himself as editor, might be undertaken with every assurance of success. Every earlier American venture had failed; the Boston *Massachusetts Magazine* (1789-1796) under Isaiah Thomas and the Philadelphia *Columbian Magazine* (1786-1790) under Mathew Carey had enjoyed somewhat brilliant careers in the two literary centers of the United States, but popular support never rallied to sustain these or dozens of similar enterprises. Undeterred, Brown described to

Armitt in December, 1799, the prospect of financial gain:

> Eight of my friends here, men in the highest degree respectable for literature and influence, have urged me so vehemently to undertake the project of a magazine and promised their contributions and assistance to its success that I have written and published proposals. Four hundred subscribers will repay the annual expense of sixteen hundred dollars. As soon as this number is obtained, the printers will begin and trust to punctual payment of these for reimbursement. All above four hundred will be clear profit to me; one thousand subscribers will produce four thousand five hundred dollars, and deducting the annual expense will leave two thousand seven hundred. If this sum is attainable, in a year or two you will allow that my prospect is consoling. The influence of my friends and their unexpected and uncommon zeal inspire me with a courage which I should be unable to derive from any other quarter.

These dreams of affluence were similar to those of other editors. Eleven years earlier Noah Webster had risked the income from his famous spelling book upon the *American Magazine*. In spite of its liveliness, its critical integrity, and its variety of matter, the magazine failed. Brown reckoned ill when he discounted the frailty of gentlemen with literary interests but with no experience in writing. Nearly every person feels that he possesses wisdom enough to write great books, but the energy, the force of style, and the ability to stare down a blank sheet of paper are seldom possessed by many well-meaning individuals. Brown was to discover that issue after issue had to be lifted either from foreign periodicals or composed by himself alone. He seems to have written in many different styles with a view to persuading his friends to follow one of these standards, and he initiated several series of periodical essays to stimulate men of varying interests to continue in the same vein.

An editor's task should be to choose from a variety of materials offered by a large number of authors; Brown had this notion. Forty years later Emerson discovered to his sorrow that even the members of the Transcendental Club could not be trusted to supply a steady flow of original prose and verse.

Brown overestimated the willingness of the young nation to support a magazine: Four dollars and fifty cents was a great deal of hard cash in a day when the major portion of American business was conducted on a barter system. Country lawyers, physicians, and preachers, whose homes and tables indicated affluent circumstances, seldom handled money. They bartered labor and foodstuffs for professional services. There being little wealth other than property, the estate of a rich person could not easily be converted to cash. By 1800 some improvement in the wide distribution of the circulating medium had taken place, but generally it was not an easy matter to persuade a thousand people to surrender silver or gold in return for a promise of a monthly magazine.

The city of New York was not large enough to support a magazine. Benjamin Rush had explained to Noah Webster the unwillingness of people in the wilderness cities to permit New York to assume a cultural superiority over the remainder of the nation.

Regionalism, provincialism, or colonialism prevented the ready acceptance of a Manhattan oracle. Brown seems not to have recognized the problem involved in attaining a national acceptance for his magazine. Smith had done well with the *Medical Repository* because of the professional aspirations of physicians in every state. The appeal of a general magazine was to the literate class as a whole. As long as that class drew its sustenance mainly from theological, legal, and medical tomes, and as long as American miscellaneous periodical essays merely aped those in the British magazines, the average citizen as well as the rich and college-educated minority found little reason to subscribe. Studies of the reading habits of college graduates today reveal that an astonishing percentage of men and women do not subscribe to a single serious periodical or engage in activities of an intellectual character outside their professional calling. Little wonder that Brown's dream of a thousand subscribers seemed utopian.

Not to be overlooked is the fact that Brown foresaw an affluence matching that of his successful merchant brothers. Possibly he was using this argument defensively; he may have dulled the edge of their disagreement by these illusory hopes of financial independence. In good Quaker fashion the Brown family stressed the importance of money. For a dozen years the novelist had scorned gold; he had lived in New York as if money did not exist, says Dunlap, or at least as if he were not under compulsion to account for his expenditures. Now, as his brothers Joseph, Armitt, and James reported increasing incomes from their successful mercantile activities, Charles insisted upon the pecuniary

advantages to be gained from the profession of writing.
It is an interesting commentary upon Brown's career
that, within a few months of the publication of his first
novel, *Wieland,* for which he took a down payment of
fifty dollars, the hope of monetary rewards reaching
thousands annually served to justify his literary career.
The American mercantile spirit never revealed itself
any more clearly than that this young man, independently well off in a wealthy family and by instinct a
hater of materialism, should have been reminded that
dollars make the mare go and that success is sweetest
when measured by the clink of coin dropping in a
strongbox.

The Monthly Magazine and American Review began in April, 1799, and ran through three volumes of
six issues each until December, 1800. The issues usually
appeared about the fifteenth of the month following
the announced date of publication. When the yellow
fever epidemic caused the editor to withdraw to Upper
New York State, the sixth issue carried the date Sep-
tember-December, and thus the first volume was completed in the calendar year 1799. Late in 1800, after a
year's effort had failed to bring sufficient subscribers,
the following announcement described a plan for altering the magazine to a quarterly:

The thin population of the United States renders
it impossible to procure sufficient support from one
city; and the dispersed situations of readers, the embarrassments attending the diffusion of copies over a
wide extent of country, and the obstacles to a prompt
collection of the small sums which so cheap a publication demanded, are, it is presumed, sufficient reasons
for altering and contracting the publication.

The *Monthly Magazine* deserved to live. Each issue of eighty pages contained the following departments: "Original"—essays and stories, many from the pen of Brown; "American Review"—critical notices of American publications; "Selections"—scientific and literary intelligence clipped or translated from foreign publications; and "Miscellaneous Articles of Literary and Philosophical Intelligence"—brief notes about authors and forthcoming books. The bipartisan nature of American politics had already rendered political discussion dangerous. The editor announced, "There already exists a sufficient number of vehicles of political discussion, . . . and it is presumed that readers in general will be best pleased with a performance limited to scientific and literary topics." Religious polemics likewise were taboo. Nothing strikes the modern reader as more curious than the total elimination from the pages of early general magazines of all topical and controversial subjects and of almost all social data relating to immigration, the westward movement, and abolition.

The selections ran the gamut from speculative essays on astronomy to practical how-to-do items like the method of removing garlic from milk. Biographical sketches of famous men and women ranged from Louis XIV to Schiller, Bürger, and Kotzebue. Elihu Hubbard Smith's essays on the Connecticut Wits were rescued from among his papers, and the five major poets —John Trumbull, Timothy Dwight, Joel Barlow, Lemuel Hopkins, and David Humphreys—were characterized.

The reviews and original essays on literary topics, most of which were written by Brown, are among the most notable in early national American literature. A concern for the literary reputation of the United States overshadowed the other interests of the paper. It must be remembered that *literature* and *learning* were almost identical terms in the eighteenth and early nineteenth centuries; a plea for better literature therefore was usually a plea for better education or a better means of attaining correct information. The term *literature* has been narrowed in recent usage to denote *belles lettres*. An essay in the first issue complained that certain conditions lessen American dignity by leading learned foreigners to remark that "the literary character of America is extremely superficial." American preoccupation with the pursuit of gain diverts attention from books and learning. Colleges and universities are little more than "mere diploma manufactories"; an earnest student can find few scholars with whom to compete. Distinguished literary attainment can expect very little reward.

Another essay examined the lack of American authorship:

I am desirous of knowing the cause of this want of authorship among us. Four millions of persons, generally taught to read and not overpowered with the barbarism of Algonquin savages or the indigence of Polish serfs, have tailors, carpenters, and even lawyers among them, but not one author can be found. Is this deficiency a proof of refinement or stupidity? Is it a topic of congratulation or condolence?

By such means Americans were urged to support education and native publications. Not until twenty years later did Washington Irving, James Fenimore Cooper, and William Cullen Bryant emerge as authentic literary figures of international stature. To no small extent their American audience had been prepared by the groundwork of nationalists like Brown.

The book reviews drew their subjects chiefly from pamphlets. The death of Washington in December, 1799, gave occasion for dozens of tributes in verse and prose, each of which was sent to the editor, who discussed them in terms of the possibility of creating a national literature out of "such stuff." Brown's head ached as he read these effusions; at last, his patience exhausted, he flayed John Searson's "Mount Vernon," a particularly bathetic poem:

The intellectual drivelings of a harmless simpleton excite, by turns, our laughter and our pity; but the printer who can employ his press to "turn" such stuff "to shape" and to give to ineffable nonsense "a local habitation and a name" deserves reprehension from all who feel a reverence for the dignity of literature. . . . When strangers light upon such volumes in our houses, smoothly bound and brightly lettered, what idea will they form of American taste?

A similar scathing comment upon *Poems* by Samuel Low provoked a controversy in the columns of the New York *Mercantile Advertiser* and its weekly, the *Spectator*, on November 15, 1800. The poet was irked by a denial that first efforts are to be praised merely because they are first efforts or because they are American.

In the final issue of the *Monthly Magazine* Brown rationalized America's attitude toward its own publications. The Preface to William Cliffton's *Poems* complained that in America genius is neglected and quackery is exalted, that "an universal irruption of Gothicism hath overpowered and decomposed" American energies, and that an utter apathy and perfect indifference to learning and works of genius pervade all ranks. These exaggerations merely expanded verses addressed by Cliffton to William Gifford:

> *In these cold shades, beneath these shifting skies*
> *Where Fancy sickens and where Genius dies,*
> *Where few and feeble are the muses' strains*
> *And no fine frenzy riots in the veins,*
> *There still are found a few to whom belong*
> *The fire of virtue and the soul of song.*

To these charges Brown rejoined forcefully. Such complaints had grown stale; it was time to face the facts. American authors fare no worse than Europeans of equal ability. The difference lies in America's quicker perception of charlatanry and in its quite natural refusal to console the vanity of incompetent writers. Authorship should not be pursued by men seeking a fortune; let them enter "the direct avenue to wealth and power."

Yet there was no real reason for despair. Brown himself had published four vigorous novels. Brackenridge had pictured the shortcomings of democracy in *Modern Chivalry,* while Mrs. Fannie Wood and other writers were basing novels upon American incidents. Noah Webster, Benjamin Rush, Francis Hopkinson, and Thomas Jefferson had written notable volumes of essays. Royall Tyler had written a play and a novel.

Dwight, Barlow, and Freneau had written worthy native poetry. A despairing attitude was as untrue as it was unwarranted; although sales may not have been large, the productions of all these authors found a fit audience. Local histories were being written in every state. Societies for stimulating research were being organized. Surely, to one reviewing these many evidences of American scholarship, America was not barren of genius nor unwilling to foster creative activity.

In commentaries upon fiction Brown repeatedly stressed the high calling of the serious prose novelist who through imaginative insight and perception of truth could give universal significance to a series of incidents drawn from everyday experience. The highest form of narrative art is the epic poem. Of the thousands of such poems attempted in all languages, only a baker's dozen are memorable. Most of the attempts had been made by persons unskilled in story telling, persons who had assumed that poetic composition is different from prose composition in being subject to an entirely different set of basic rules. The fact is, of course, that both poetry and prose must use words, sentences, and figures of speech in identical patterns. The themes and purposes are identical. The significant difference lies in the addition of meter or "numbers," and the more extensive use of tone color in poetry. On the oft-debated subject of the comparative merits of prose and verse as vehicles for narratives, Brown had this to say in a review of Robert Southey's *Joan of Arc:*

The selection of a theme truly important, adorning it with the luster of eloquence, supplying with judicious hand the deficiencies of history in the statement of motives and the enumeration of circumstances, fashioning falsehood by the most rigid standard of probability, and suggesting to the readers beneficial truths is the sublimest province that can be assigned to man. It is questionable whether verse be a more advantageous garb of such a theme than prose; but whatever superiority we ascribe to verse, this superiority is small. All that constitutes the genuine and lasting excellence of narratives, all the subtilties of ratiocination, the energies and ornaments of rhetoric, and the colors of description are compatible with prose. Numbers are an equivocal or at least not an essential attribute of a moral and useful tale.

The original materials in the *Monthly Magazine* are especially notable for short stories and serialized novels from the pen of Brown. The first issue contains a fragment of *Edgar Huntly* and "On Apparitions," a Gothic tale of a Hungarian who brings into a man's presence a dead friend. "Walstein's School of History," supposedly from the German of Krantz of Gotha (August and September, 1799), which summarizes the first part of *Arthur Mervyn*, has the effect of being a self-criticism, for the fictitious German author's name apparently is a metaphor by which Brown asserts that he has won the laurel wreath of pre-eminence in Gothic fiction. Since there is a reference to the study of German in the "Dialogues of the Living," these tales reveal the editor's growing interest in the new German literature.

Best known of Brown's short stories is "Thessalonica: A Roman Story" (May, 1799), an illustration of the maxim, "No diligence or moderation can fully restrain the passions of the multitude." Set in Salonika at the conclusion of the Gothic War in A.D. 390, the story concerns the hatred existing between the Roman army of occupation and the populace. Soldiers deny permission to Macro to enter the senators' gate at the theater; in the altercation he is injured. Mob violence flares, and many civilians and soldiers are killed. A truce is patched up, but later at a religious festival when a dart kills a charioteer, the soldiers butcher every person in the hippodrome. Again, as in "The Death of Cicero," Brown chose horror materials implicit in actual historical data. Although the point is not specifically stated, the story illustrates the conventional American fear of a standing army as a provoker of discord.

"Portrait of an Emigrant" (June, 1799) tells of a Frenchman with a half-Negro wife; both work in Philadelphia and give a rare example of "unmingled and uninterrupted felicity." Since this tale has the epigrammatic quality of Brown, it doubtless is his, for it is signed "B." "The Household: A Fragment" (August, 1800) gives a fictional family history in the fashion found in the novels; it too seems to be by Brown. "The Trials of Arden" (July, 1800), "Friendship" (July, 1800), and "Original Letters" (August, 1800) also seem to be by Brown.

Quite certainly by Brown is "A Lesson on Concealment; or, Memoirs of Mary Selwyn" (March, 1800), a novelette of a woman who, required by her family to wed Colmer, falls in love with Hayward. When she learns that Hayward has a wife, she runs away to Ridgefield, Connecticut. Here after the birth of a child and unsuccessful efforts to commit suicide, she meets Molesworth, a man "weary of the turbulence and vices of the city." Believing that she will not be discovered, she marries Molesworth. When they move to the city, she sees Hayward and becomes terror-stricken. She learns that Hayward had killed her brother in a duel when the latter sought "vengeance for his sister's honor." Mary dies without explaining to Molesworth the reasons for her distraction. The moral of the tale is apparent: by concealing the true state of her affections and the reasons for her disappearance from home, she created much unhappiness and led to her brother's death. Although she had said, "O! how blest are those whose conduct is exempt from parental or fraternal dominion, who are suffered to consult the dictates of their reason, and are not driven by imperious duties to the sacrifice of liberty and the death of honor," the story is directed less at the error of parents in requiring obedience than at the error of concealing one's conduct and true nature. This theme of concealment recurs frequently in Brown's fiction and affords in this respect an interesting link between his work and that of Hawthorne.

The most important single work by Brown in the *Monthly Magazine* is "Memoirs of Stephen Calvert" (June, 1799-June, 1800), which he had begun energetically in 1798, but which he had dropped with the conception of *Ormond*. "Stephen Calvert" was written serially during the period of publication. In February, 1800, the story lapsed. To a reader who wittily complained about the cessation of the novel just as Calvert "snatched his hat from the table and whipped out of the room," Brown answered: "The narrative of Cal-

vert was interrupted for good reasons, with which, however, it would be absurd and impertinent to tease the
reader. The obstacles are now removed, and the tale
will be resumed in the ensuing number, and punctually
continued."

This work, ostensibly the first part of a five-part
novel, completes one major episode in the life of
Stephen Calvert, a British-born youth of eighteen whose
parents took up residence in America when he was a
child. The story opens with Calvert, weary of the
evils of society, seeking solitude in the Territory of
Ohio on the banks of Lake Michigan. A long backward
loop to England details the history of his family since
1642, the separation of himself and his twin brother,
the removal of his father to America, and Stephen's
education.

Once this complicated beginning is passed, the reader
comes upon a highly interesting study of a young
man's vacillation in love. After deciding to wed the
diminutive, unattractive Louisa Calvert, who is beloved by Sidney Carlton, Stephen meets Clelia Neville.
She greets his proposal of marriage with a shriek, for
she has confused him with the long-lost twin brother for
whom she fled from a loveless marriage to the de-
praved Belgrade in Ireland. At this point the novel
ends inconclusively; yet there is a hint that Stephen
ultimately causes the death of Louisa and that he
becomes a villain of the darkest hue.

"Memoirs of Stephen Calvert," though never issued
separately as a book, in some respects is one of Brown's
better novels, deserving a place with *Wieland* and
Edgar Huntly for its focus upon a few characters dur-

ing a brief interval of time and for poetic allusiveness. In addition to the psychologizing and the cerebral quality notable in the four more famous novels, it has a larger share of conversation. The background description is, as always, quite inadequate, while the genealogical history of the Calvert family is too extensive. The substance of the novel is close to ordinary life: its main ingredients have to do with a youth's seeking wealth through marriage and with his inability to decide between dutiful wedlock to an unattractive girl and selfishly pleasureful union with a beautiful lady. The unexpected complication by means of a twin brother certainly is less remarkable than ventriloquism and sleepwalking; yet Brown manages the plot sufficiently well to declare: "Strange incidents they are, and such as, I believe, have now occurred for the first time in the history of human beings."

Primarily illustrated is the theme that an ardent youth requires the guidance of experience rather than of speculation. Unhardened by the fires of rigorous accountability for his deeds, a young man too readily bends with every fleeting emotion. Even a mind fastidious in its choice of principles of conduct may commit error, because each new pretty face and each new turn of events can imperceptibly cause the alteration of principles or aims. Brown in part reflects in this novel his drift toward authority: just as in *Ormond* he concludes that rationalism unbased in the fixed principles of religion may lead to error, so "Stephen Calvert" illustrates the folly of trusting large decisions to emotionally unstable and inexperienced youth. Wisdom in leadership results from a combination of humanitarian impulses with a moderation approved by custom. Some attention is given in relation to the main theme to anti-slavery and to the controversy between Protestantism and Roman Catholicism. The second major theme is concealment. Brown shows how delay makes the disclosure of the truth more difficult, how easily artifices and subterfuges undermine faith, and how the fear of humiliation rises feverishly as a sense of guilt increases. Stephen's conduct toward Louisa, as he well knows, is wholly reprehensible.

The maxims are less sharply condensed in "Memoirs of Stephen Calvert" than in the earlier novels, but their effectiveness is not diminished as a result of the expanded phrasing of general truths concerning conduct, the emotions, and man's place in the universe. Here are four of the more interesting examples:

There is an energy in the human mind which enables it to conquer every inquietude, or a flexibility that reconciles itself to every constraint.

On how slender threads does the destiny of human beings frequently depend! The caprice of a moment, an inexplicable and transitory impulse, in consequence of which our steps move one inch forward or on one side, will sometimes ascertain the tenor of our whole life, will influence the happiness and govern the activity of one man, and through life control the destiny of nations and the world.

Time hushes every storm, and, when the hurricane has ended its career, every flowing of the billows is less impetuous than the last; till at length the tranquilizing power "summa placidum caput extulit unda." Thus it is in the tempests of the mind. Hope breaks through the cloud which hung over us and shut out the day, and brings back serenity and radiance.

The world is eternally producing what to our precipitate judgment are prodigies, anomalies, monsters. Innate, dastardly, sordid wickedness frequently springs up where genial temperature and wise culture had promised us the most heavenly products. The ruffian and sensualist are fashioned by the discipline intended and, as the fond preceptor dreams, adapted to produce nothing but generous magnanimity and heroism.

Clara Howard & Jane Talbot

AT THE end of the eighteenth century Charles Brockden Brown was the most considerable man of letters in New York. As the author of four impressive novels and as the editor of a notable literary magazine, he gave promise of becoming the writer who would prove to a skeptical world that Americans were not degenerating into orangoutangs. Buffon, the French naturalist, had popularized the convenient notion that, since Europe had reached the zenith of cultivation, emigrants to the wilds of America must necessarily decline into animality. European travelers looked for signs of uncouthness indicative of barbarism. Americans, on the other hand, spied genius in every native sermon, verse, painting, musical composition, scientific observation, and mechanical gadget. National self-respect had been piqued. Europe snubbed American pretensions by asking for evidence of native Chaucers, Spensers, Shakespeares, and Miltons. In response, Dwight, Barlow, and Freneau had soared upon Icarian epic flights; even the youthful Brown had tried his wings. Theologians cut ancient fetters. Well might the Reverend Samuel Miller write *A Brief Retrospect of the Eighteenth Century* to show that the United States was keeping pace intellectually with Europe. A small population scattered through more than a hundred thousand square miles of territory was justifiably proud of superb achievements in politics, in natural science, in art, and in literature. Brown was the first American novelist is to be hailed as a genius.

When the sad news came that General Washington had died, the city of New York solemnly draped its houses with symbols of mourning. Dunlap closed the theater. At its reopening on Monday evening, December 30, 1799, Thomas Abthorpe Cooper, the actor, spoke a "Monody on the Death of George Washington." The author of this elegy was Brown, chosen for the honor both by reason of his friendship with Dunlap and his eminence as an author. Unhappily Cooper's artificial and declamatory recitation drew hisses from the gallery and groans from the pit as he fumbled sixty or seventy lines. Crito, whose dramatic criticisms irked the actors, poked fun at Cooper in the New York *Commercial Advertiser* on January 1, 1800. The poem as printed in this same issue of the newspaper contained ninety-eight lines. The actor immediately demanded that his name be cleared; Brown on the following day announced that some "thirty lines were added anew to the copy sent to the press, which were wanting in that which was prepared for the stage." The poem was also published in the January, 1800, issue of the *Monthly Magazine*.

The poem laments the passing of Washington, the friend of all people in all lands. Instead of weeping at his demise, the populace is urged to sing hymns of praise that Heaven permitted this mortal so long a life; without his unifying force as President the youthful land might have lost the liberty he bestowed upon his countrymen:

> *Thus, after foes subdued and battles done,*
> *The harder task was his, to make us one:*
> *The seeds to crush with his pacific hand*
> *By home-bred discord scattered through the land.*
> *'Twas he, the darling child of bounteous fate,*
> *That rear'd aloft the pillar of our state;*
> *'Twas he that fixed upon eternal base*
> *The freedom, peace, and glory of his race.*

This verse lacks emotional and imaginative lift. Although there were few better tributes to Washington written at the time, the monody demonstrates anew that Brown's forte was prose.

The magazine continued to engross Brown throughout the year 1800. Especially attentive was he to the section entitled "American Review," for the plan of passing judgment upon every new publication in the United States seemed useful in the creation of a national literary reputation. Many persons deemed American authors too thin-skinned to endure a truthful analysis of their esthetic and intellectual shortcomings. America is a youthful land, it was commonly asserted; adverse criticism must await the time when American writers will have enjoyed the same background of cultivation and leisure found in the older European nations. Brown disliked this attitude which demanded praise for good intentions instead of censure of shortcomings. In a day when no other American came forward to lay down principles of literary merit, he did so. He takes his place as one of the first important critics in the United States, not so much because he originated or exemplified criteria for a new national literature, but because by energy and priority he tried to distinguish between work that was honest and dishonest, interesting and dull, competent and incompetent.

When he wrote to his brother James in April, Charles quite naturally was concerned with problems of bookmaking in the United States. Because Maxwell proved dilatory and reluctant in the fulfillment of his promises, James recommended that the second part of *Arthur Mervyn* be issued in New York rather than Philadelphia. Charles followed his brother's advice by making arrangements with George F. Hopkins, a printer and bookseller. James had evidently taken considerable interest in the marketing of Charles' wares, as well as in the "gloominess and out-of-nature incidents," for the latter wrote: "Book making, as you observe, is the dullest of all trades, and the utmost that any American can look for in his native country is to be reimbursed in his unavoidable expenses." He added, "The saleability of my works will much depend upon their popularity in England, whither Caritat has carried a considerable number of *Wieland, Ormond,* and *Mervyn.*" James steadily placed pressure on Charles to test success by financial reward.

Joseph, the eldest brother whose residence was in

Edenton, North Carolina, visited family friends in Philadelphia and Princeton, New Jersey, in the summer of 1800. Charles journeyed homeward to join the family circle; on the way he passed agreeable days with friends at New Brunswick. Joseph invited Charles to accompany him to the southward, but Charles remarked: "I am reluctant to comply. I know not why, scarcely. Seldom less happy than at present. Seldom has my prospect been a gloomier one. Yet it may shine when least expected."

The melancholy tone of Brown's comments may have derived from a recurrence of ill health, or again there may have been ineffectual efforts to woo a maid and win a wife. Dunlap hints as much in printing this undated quotation: "My conception of the delights and benefits connected with love and marriage are exquisite. They have swayed most of my thoughts and many of my actions since I arrived at an age of reflection and maturity. They have given birth to the sentiment of love with regard to several women. Mutual circumstances have frustrated the natural operations of that sentiment in several instances. At present I am free. None of those with whom I have recently associated have any claims upon me, nor have I any upon them."

Late in 1800 Brown fell in love with Miss Elizabeth Linn, eldest daughter of the Reverend William Linn, a Presbyterian preacher in New York City. Not until four years later did the wedding take place. The motives for delay can merely be conjectured. Certainly the sectarian objections of Brown's Quaker parents were stated, as they had been in the affair with Miss Potts. Yet other more powerful reasons must have operated to delay the event so long. Possibly Brown's recurring melancholy threw too deep a shade for Miss Linn to penetrate.

On September 1, 1800, Brown wrote to R. P., an unidentified correspondent, a letter containing unmistakable hints of low vitality. He had returned to Philadelphia "not to see different scenes, to breathe different airs, but merely to see a different set of faces. I stayed in Jersey—at Newark, Brunswick, and Princeton—half a week, and now I have come back to my ancient neighborhood." He continued:

All the inanimate objects in this city are uniform, monotonous, and dull. I have been surprised at the little power they have over my imagination, at the sameness that every where reigns. A nine months' absence has cast upon surrounding objects not a gleam of novelty. All the old impressions seem to exist with their pristine freshness in my memory. Under this sun I discover nothing new, but this sameness pleases not. More irksome, more deadening to my fancy is this city on its *own* account than ever. I am puzzled to guess how it happens, but it is of little moment to inquire, since walls and pavements were never anything to me or at least were next to nothing, social and intellectual pleasures being every thing.

To this correspondent he confessed that their friendship had been marred by his conduct in the preceding November; he had been unreasonably reserved because "something lay heavy on my heart" and because his friend had accounted for his silence in an unflattering way. With that strange inability to speak forthrightly which had marked his relationship with Smith

and Dunlap, Brown admitted that "a fantastic apprehension" withheld him from revealing the idea which
spread a cloud over him.

Upon the completion of the third volume in December, 1800, *The Monthly Magazine and American
Review* was rechristened *The American Review and
Literary Journal,* which was issued as a quarterly. Reviews of American books now occupied the key position
in each issue, and original essays were relegated to the
last pages. At the end of every six months a half-
yearly retrospect surveyed political events and remarkable occurrences in America; work on this section
paved the way for Brown's political pamphleteering
and annal writing. Like its predecessor, this magazine
rose above the party spirit dividing the supporters of
John Adams and Thomas Jefferson.

Nearly every article in the new magazine was an
original review based upon American and foreign publications. No similar periodical had been attempted in
America. To the task of compilation, Brown and his
associates brought the fearless impartiality that had
marked the parent magazine. In accord with contemporary custom, books were summarized at length, and
large sections were excerpted; but books were not made
the basis of new interpretations of subject matter in
the manner of some British magazines. "Our purpose,"
wrote the editor, "is not so much to exhibit our own
opinion as the spirit and manner of the authors themselves."

The *American Review* closed its career in the autumn
of 1802 at the end of its second year of publication.
Brown's share in the magazine has never been clearly

determined. Some scholars have thought that Brown's return to Philadelphia in 1801 severed his connection with the New York magazines. Yet a letter to John Blair Linn on July 8, 1802, contained these significant sentences: "The review is exceedingly behind hand, and my friends have imposed on me the task of reading and reviewing half a dozen books, which without their injunctions I should never have looked into. This has been an irksome undertaking which nothing but a kind of necessity could reconcile me to."

When Brown returned to Philadelphia early in 1801, he resided with his brother James and joined the importing firm of his brothers James and Armitt. The risk was great, but the profits of a successful voyage were immense. To Miss Linn, who asked for a description of his business activities, Charles wrote on December 7, 1802: "You hint at the propriety of my unbosoming myself upon my affairs. What hitherto has deterred me? Nothing but the sense that the detail of my affairs would be unintelligible. The general truths —that I have an equal share in the gains of my profession with my brothers; that those gains were, one and two years ago, such as to secure thee and me in the possession of affluence. I have often told you misfortunes (I have not concealed from thee) have since come, and now what remains but to build up again the half-fallen edifice: not to suffer the disappointments of the highest hopes to extinguish Hope altogether." This last sentence doubtless refers to their marriage plans. The final known reference to the business occurs in a letter to Miss Linn on March 25, 1804: "What sad news has this day brought. Some three months ago we sent a vessel to St. Domingo with a valuable cargo; a young man, our particular friend and kinsman, the hope and joy of a numerous and worthy family, went as supercargo. This day tells us that he and the captain are both dead, and by their death the vessel and cargo, worth $15,000, are probably lost and certainly exposed to great delay and imminent risk." Charles' share in the business seems to have been that of an investor with only slight office duties. The firm was dissolved in 1806.

It is possible that Brown assisted his father in the work of conveyancing, for on May 4, 1802, he wrote of the desire of Robert Cumming to terminate amicably a suit instituted by a Mr. Dawson. In the spring of 1802 Grandmother Armitt died, she who was so devoted to the unpredictable lad with a craving for eminence in literature. Her will, probated on April 26, provided that her dwelling house, furniture, and plate, "except what is before given to my grandson Charles Brockden Brown," should be held in trust for her daughter Mary Brown, the novelist's mother. Her son-in-law Richard Waln and her grandson Charles Brockden Brown were named as executors. It would appear, therefore, that in the grandmother's eyes Charles had distinguished himself beyond his brothers and deserved both the gifts already bestowed and the commission accruing from his duties as executor. Of course, one might also remark cynically that Grandmother Armitt used this method to assist an otherwise improvident grandson, but a fair interpretation of the whole family friendship, as it is pieced together from the few surviving documents, belies such an unkind view.

Brown's business activities engrossed but a portion of his time. Writing was still his chief vocation. Although his point of view was slowly being changed by association with his brothers, he yet preferred authorship to any other profession. John Davis, the British traveler, reported a visit in June, 1801: "At Philadelphia I found Mr. Brown, who felt no remission of his literary diligence by a change of his abode. He was ingratiating himself into the favor of the ladies by writing a new novel, and rivaling Lopez de Vega by the multitude of his works. . . . Mr. Brown said little, but seemed lost in meditation; his creative fancy was perhaps conjuring up scenes to spin out the thread of his new novel."

This new novel was *Clara Howard; In a Series of Letters*, which was published by Asbury Dickins in Philadelphia on July 2, 1801. It was reprinted in London in 1807 with the title *Philip Stanley; or, The Enthusiasm of Love*, and the hero's name was changed from Edward Harley to Philip Stanley. American reprints by Samuel G. Goodrich in 1827, Moses Pollock in 1857, and David McKay in 1887 adopted the title *Clara Howard; or, The Enthusiasm of Love* and retained the hero's new name.

Clara Howard, an epistolary romance, shows what happened to Brown's fiction when he avoided "out-of-nature incidents" and dark-hued villains. The pithy sentences remain, skillful plot structure survives, nerve-tingling suspense still enchains interest, but by comparison with its predecessors the novel is uninteresting. The letter device reduces almost to the vanishing point the use of conversation and descriptive detail. Brown summarizes the narrative in expository fashion. The characters become two-dimensional puppets illustrating the clichés that "sweet are the uses of adversity" and "it is foolish to grow despondent under the most unfavorable circumstances."

Philip Stanley is a young watchmaker's apprentice who has been tutored by an elderly friend, Mr. E. Howard. Desiring to become a universal benefactor, much as did Arthur Mervyn, Philip seeks a wife with money. He is willing to wed the unattractive Mary Wilmot, but when the more wealthy Clara appears, he shifts his affections. Inadvertently he mentions Mary's name, and Clara requires him to seek Mary and, if her happiness requires it, to marry her. In his search Philip nearly dies rescuing a drowning child. At last, despairing of success, he plans to embark on a voyage to China. Mary reappears and explains that she is in love with Sedley. The four young people prepare for a double wedding. Philip's fiery, impetuous spirit goes willingly under the protective wing of the high-minded Clara.

Brown rightly named the novel after the heroine, for she dominates the action by bending Philip to her will. She insists that "the welfare of another may demand self-denial from us, and that in bestowing benefits on others there is purer delight than in gratifications merely selfish and exclusive." She believes it her duty to resign Philip to Mary, because she will "derive more satisfaction from disinterested than from selfish conduct." She estimates people not by their wealth but by their intrinsic qualities of heart and head. Clara is, therefore, a rationalist of the school of Constantia Dudley in *Ormond.*

The main theme of the novel is: Wealth is desirable as a means of attaining happiness, but marriage merely to secure money is unwise; love alone must determine one's decision. Mary Wilmot rejects Sedley until her trials bring forcibly to her attention the true qualities of this rich man; when her emotions and her reason find Sedley acceptable, she yields. Philip realizes his error in choosing Mary merely for her money; when love coincides with his ambitions, he can do no other than claim Clara as a bride and try to fulfill her strange prescription for happiness. The secondary theme is "the impiety of despair." The four main characters have moments when existence seems melancholy enough to make death a pleasant outlet to life's sorrow. Yet in each person's life the dark clouds vanish in the bright sunshine of happiness.

In *Clara Howard,* Brown tossed aside his most distinctive and his most attractive substance. Gone is abnormal psychology, including sex perversion and evil manifesting itself in brutal force and in diabolical intellectual cunning; gone are those strange medical phenomena of ventriloquism, sleepwalking, identity of fate in twins, spontaneous combustion of humans, and epidemic disease; and gone are the wild elements of nature—the red man and the panther. Horror and terror, not love and romance, were Brown's proper precinct. By withdrawing from the areas of terror, he became merely another purveyor of romantic narrative. However close to Bage and Godwin he remained in his moralizing, he lost the Gothic excitement which had given strength and interest to his better books. Moralizing could be found in virtually every peri-

odical essay and sermon; spine-chilling narrative focus-
ing attention upon a single climax was rare in any literature. Meritorious though the novel is, it lacks that
hair-raising compulsiveness and originality which make
Wieland and *Edgar Huntly* minor classics.

Immediately upon the publication of *Clara Howard*,
Brown and William Coleman took the popular cruise
up the Hudson River to Albany. As the boat withdrew from the wharf in New York on July 7, 1801,
the novelist meditated upon the course of events which
had been so various and momentous in his life since
he first reached the metropolis. His conclusion was
that some of his experiences were "humiliating and disastrous but on the whole leading me to my present situation in which I have reason for congratulation." On
July 10 at Red Hook, Brown recorded a familiar
symptom: "Heavy brows and languid blood have made
me indolent, and I have done nothing but look about
me or muse for the last two days." A walk ashore
while the boat was docked gave some relief from
sluggish feelings. Reading matter was scarce, and Brown
sampled the captain's stock of books, which consisted
of Dilworth's *Arithmetic* and Oliver Goldsmith's *Citizen of the World*. The latter did not please Brown:
"The fiction is ill supported, the style smooth and
elegant, but the sentiments and observations far from
judicious or profound." The mate beguiled the jaded
traveler with tales of visits to Nootka, Canton, and
Greenland.

From Albany, Brown proceeded to Lebanon, Nor-
thampton, Hartford, New Haven, and New York. Of
Lebanon he said: "The scenery around is sweetly pic-

holy names. Inquiry is not a sign of disbelief, and inquirers are not necessarily bad. Says Jane, "I find it possible for men to disbelieve and yet retain their claims to our reverence, our affection, and especially our good offices." She is certain that association with Colden has made her a better woman: "Not only my piety has become more rational and fervent, but a new spring has been imparted to my languishing curiosity." Supported by such sympathy, Colden during his long exile has abundant opportunity for reviewing his opinions: "The incidents of a long voyage, the vicissitudes through which I have passed, have given strength to my frame, while the opportunities and occasions for wisdom which these have afforded me have made my mind whole. I have awakened from my dreams of doubt and misery, not to the cold and vague belief, but to the living and delightful consciousness of every tie that can bind man to his Divine Parent and Judge." And Colden promises to be "no mean example and no feeble teacher" of these lessons.

Brown's investigation of varieties of religious belief comes to a satisfying conclusion in *Jane Talbot*. Theodore Wieland represents an excess of enthusiasm which perverts the mind and leads to dangerous mania; Constantia Dudley demonstrates that an absence of religious principles even in a strong-minded rationalist may lead to terrifying errors; Jane Talbot and Henry Colden make clear the necessity for a harmony of intellectually achieved religious beliefs to make a socially acceptable and, possibly, a happy marriage. Brown here recognizes that religious "measles" are part of the growing pains of life; he does not denounce unbelief but rather he attempts to help the reader understand the process of arriving at an intellectually defensible religious faith. *Jane Talbot* may have been an outgrowth of Brown's association with the Reverend John Blair Linn, brother of his betrothed and a pastor of a Philadelphia church. The adjustment Brown himself had to make to enter the Presbyterian divine's family may have been written into fiction.

Despite its slight plot, *Jane Talbot* provided an opportunity for sententiousness:

All happiness springs from affection; nature ordains no tie so strong as that between the sexes; to love without bounds is to confer bliss not only on ourselves but on another; conjugal affection is the genuine sphere not only of happiness but duty.

Women feel deeply but boast not. The supposed indecency of forwardness makes their words generally fall short of their sentiments; and passion, when once thoroughly imbibed, is as hard to be escaped from as it was difficultly acquired.

There is no crime which remorse will not expiate, and no more shining virtue in the whole catalogue than sincerity.

Trifling distinctions and minute subtleties make one Christian the mortal foe of another, while in their social conduct there is no difference to be found between them.

The esteem of the good is only of less value in my eyes than the approbation of my own conscience.

Experience is the antidote of wonder.

In some sense the religion of the timorous and uninquisitive is true. In another sense it is false. Considering the proofs on which it reposes, it is false, since it merely originates in deference to the opinions of others, wrought into belief by means of habit. It is on a level, as to the proof which supports it, with the wildest dreams of savage superstition or the fumes of a dervish's fanaticism.

Jane Talbot was published by John Conrad and Company, a firm of Philadelphia printers and booksellers with family ties in several cities to the southward. With the parent house in Philadelphia, Brown seems to have reached an agreement to become an editor of their publications. For the first time in the United States a family of printers united to distribute each other's publications. Thus editions of Shakespeare and other writers were easily disposed of. Soon Brown would discover in this chain of stores an outlet for a profitable magazine.

Brown's pen was not idle. In addition to supplying reviews and items of literary intelligence to the *American Review*, he occasionally scribbled a verse or brief essay for Joseph Dennie's *Port Folio*, a literary weekly established in Philadelphia in 1801. Dennie allied himself with Asbury Dickins, the publisher of *Clara Howard;* these two organized the Tuesday Club, a group of Philadelphians with literary interests. Brown attended irregularly: He who might have been the literary lion of Philadelphia remained quietly in his office and home. The following lines from "The Poet's Prayer," ascribed to Brown by John E. Hall, appeared in the *Port Folio* on May 2, 1801. They reflect the mood in which Brown withdrew from society and from his career in fiction:

Charles Brockden Brown

Fame! I abjure thee, hate thee; thou hast nought
Worthy calling into life. . . . Come, blest Obscurity!
Thy numberless delights around me shed!
Give me to walk in privacy, to know
The joys that hover in thy friendly shade,
The sweet possession of a name unknown.

Political Pamphleteer

BROWN'S generalized comments upon society had avoided specific political discussion. Yet he was alert to the rapid alterations taking place in the United States. The Jeffersonians were denouncing the Federalist leaders for committing alleged acts of nepotism and for holding monarchical, aristocratic notions. Brown paused contemplatively as he observed the supporters of Jefferson in Tammany and other clubs, and as he read the editorial billingsgate flung daily by Benjamin Franklin Bache, William Greenleaf, and other Jeffersonian editors. The end often justifies the means. Brown, however, came to doubt that axiom. It seemed that Jefferson had the best principles and the worst policy, while the Federalists had the best men and the wisest leadership, as well as practical experience in large financial and political activities. The young philosopher was faced with making a choice between the old, tried followers of Washington and the newfangled notions of Jefferson.

Brown's decision was hastened and possibly determined by his return to Philadelphia to join his brothers in the importing concern. Their early success made him conscious of the prerogatives of the mercantile class. Losses at sea, occasioned partly by mischance and partly by Jefferson's naval policy, tended to embitter most shipping men against a national leadership hostile to the best interests of a great and growing commerce. Jefferson wished to withdraw ships from international trade; the Federalists insisted that the President enforce the rights of neutral ships on the high seas. Brown's brothers denounced a policy which left American ships at the mercy of marauding men-of-war, whether British or French, because Jefferson laid up under cover the few frigates constituting the American navy. John Adams had fathered the navy to support a greater merchant fleet; now American enterprise on the four seas was atrophied by a national leader whose conduct resulted in appeasement rather than in vigorous affirmative action.

The Federalists made capital of Jefferson's friendship for France. Wherever the French were near the United States, there the Federalists found danger to the Union. Particularly did they find political ammunition in the plight of the Westerners who shipped produce down the Mississippi River. The discovery in January, 1802, that Spain had retroceded Louisiana to France, a cession at first denied by Talleyrand, gave rise to many remonstrances and memorials. War was foreseen if satisfactory negotiations were not concluded. The Federalists gloated over the dilemma of the peace-loving Jefferson; late in 1802 they began a furious campaign to force his hand.

On October 18 Juan Ventura Morales, an officer of New Orleans, closed the Mississippi at New Orleans to United States vessels by abrogating the right of deposit, a right enjoyed since the Treaty of 1795. Merchandise and produce from the interior were shipped to New Orleans, stored at a moderate charge, and then reshipped in coastwise vessels. Morales' act was officially disavowed by the Spanish governor, Salcedo, but Morales was not subject to Salcedo's orders. It was apparent that, when France took over Louisiana, conditions might become even more unbearable for Americans.

From Pittsburgh to the southward newspapers published incendiary essays. Aaron Burr prepared, over the name "Coriolanus," a series of sharp letters for the New York *Morning Chronicle*. These articles advocated the immediate seizure of Louisiana as a means of safeguarding Western commerce and of preventing France from separating that region from the Union. Already the notion was abroad that to the United States must eventually belong all territory between the two oceans: "All empire," said Burr, "is traveling from East to West. Probably her last and broadest seat will be America." The mood of the moment is reflected in the following "Extract of a Letter from a Gentleman at Natchez, dated January 20, 1803," published in the Philadelphia *American Daily Advertiser* of March 7, 1803:

The reptile Spaniards act in the most hostile manner towards our citizens and commerce—with degrading remarks that the people of the United States have no national character, that they are a divided, weak, quarrelsome people without energy, and that they have nothing to fear from them. Such language is too insulting.

To give you a farther view of our aggrieved situation, I will only state that a few days since a parcel of cotton arrived at New Orleans, the bales being so damaged that it was necessary to have them repacked before being shipped. They were landed by paying 6 percent duty and cannot be reshipped on board an American vessel, but must on reshipment pay 6 percent more as Spanish produce on board a Spanish bottom. . . . I trust 700,000 persons will not wait for Mr. Jefferson to go through all the forms, ceremonies, and etiquette of the courts of Spain and Bonaparte before they determine whether it will be best to drive the miscreants from the waters or not. I say, start and drive them with the spring flood and then negotiate. We can now get the whole province without the loss of one drop of blood.

Along the Eastern seaboard, Federalists gathered in solemn convocation to denounce French-Spanish perfidy and Jeffersonian poltroonery. The New York *Evening Post* of January 8 reported: "A meeting of the merchants of Philadelphia was held to consider what steps it would be proper to pursue to obtain redress for Spanish injuries." Whether Charles Brockden Brown attended this meeting we cannot know, but the sentiment of his fellow merchants gave rise to his first partisan essay. He wrote a ninety-two-page pamphlet, *An Address to the Government of the United States on the Cession of Louisiana to the French, and on the Late Breach of Treaty by the Spaniards: Including a Translation of a Memorial, on the War of St. Domingo and Cession of the Mississippi to France,*

Drawn up by a French Counsellor of State. Issued on January 19, 1803 at fifty cents a copy, it sold out rapidly; an abridged edition of fifty-six pages at twenty-five cents was published on March 3. Newspapers throughout the nation abstracted it or reprinted portions, and John Alburtis, a printer at Martinsburg, [West] Virginia, got out an edition based on the New York *Herald's* summary for distribution to transmontane readers.

The pamphlet created a furore. Fourcroy wrote to Talleyrand from Philadelphia on January 24, saying that the pamphlet had caused a great sensation. Pichon reported from Washington, D. C., that the authorship of the pamphlet was attributed to Gouverneur Morris and Aaron Burr. The Philadelphia *Aurora*, chief Jeffersonian daily, led the assault, while Coleman's New York *Evening Post* rallied to the defense. Newspapers throughout the land took up the hue and cry. On February 10 the *Aurora* announced that the pamphlet "is the production of a novel writer of great celebrity in one of our capital cities, and this brochure was issued, not in a serious view but to try public taste in that *novel* walk of *Romance*." In another squib the author was identified as "The Man at Home," the title employed in 1798 by Brown in the Philadelphia *Weekly Magazine*. The fiction of America's first important novelist sold poorly, but the same author's political pamphlets were widely debated. It is not difficult to understand why a man, anxious to teach lessons through books to his countrymen, yielded ambition in imaginative literature when factual writing was rewarded with the headiest kind of vituperation and praise.

In the *Address* Brown used a device of fiction. He first presented—as if he were its discoverer, translator, and editor—a memorandum by a French counselor of state to Napoleon. It set forth the reasons why France, now at peace in Europe, should discontinue its war against the Negroes in St. Domingo and should instead focus its efforts upon the development of a flourishing colony at New Orleans. Since all shipping on the Mississippi River passed through this city, the French could control the vital life cord of the whole area between the two ranges of mountains south of Canada. By expanding its sphere of influence, especially through the provocation of revolts among Negro slaves against American masters and by re-enlisting the support of the Indians, France might easily acquire this vast fertile domain. This result seemed attainable because of factional strife in the loosely confederated states, and because Jefferson's Democratic Party, sympathetic with France, now ruled the United States and would pliantly acquiesce in all French schemes. "They will take pains to shut their eyes against future evils. They will be remarkably quick-sighted to the danger of a rupture with us. Their scruples against the violation of treaties and against offensive war will be wonderfully strong."

At the conclusion of this purported translation, Brown editorialized that the French counselor had made an extreme statement about America's fluctuating policy, inveterate factional strife, and inattention to the dangers possible from Negro and Indian uprisings. Yet while symptoms of these weaknesses did exist, Americans, as in 1776, would rise to repel encroachments on their liberty. Nor would any man think a renewal of all the devastations of the Revolution too great a price to give for the expulsion of foreigners from this land. "We have a *right* to the possession," declared Brown:

The interests of the human race demand from us the exertion of this right. These interests demand that the reign of peace and concord should be diffused as widely and prolonged as much as possible. By unity of manners, laws, and government is concord preserved, and this unity will be maintained with as little danger of interruption as the nature of human affairs will permit by the gradual extension of our own settlements, by erecting new communities as fast as the increase of these settlements requires it, and by sheltering them all under the pacific wing of a federal government.

To introduce a foreign nation, all on fire to extend their own power; fresh from pernicious conquests, equipped with all the engines of war and violence; measuring their own success by the ruin of their neighbors; eager to divert into channels of their own the trade and revenue which have hitherto been ours; raising an insuperable mound to our future progress; spreading among us with fatal diligence the seeds of faction and rebellion: . . . what more terrible evil can befall us? What more fatal wound to the future population, happiness, and concord of this new world? The friend of his country and of mankind must regard it with the deepest horror.

Brown recognized that lives would be lost in driving out this formidable power, but the gain would be worth all it would cost. "Our whole zeal, all our passions ought to be engaged in its success." Immediate action must be taken because Napoleon had declared,

"My designs on the Mississippi will never be officially announced till they are executed. . . . I shall trust to the folly of England and America to let me go my own way in my own time." In view of this statement, the danger seemed appalling. The transfer of Louisiana to France by Spain was a manifest breach of friendship. To drive out Spain without delay, therefore, "is a just proceeding. At least, to forbid the transfer and to prevent its execution, by forcible means if need be, is indisputably just. . . . We have looked on with stupid apathy while European powers toss about among themselves the property which God and Nature have made ours."

Brown recommended that prompt action be taken at New Orleans, and that no trust be placed in a long series of tedious negotiations: "It is for us to redress the wrong by our own power, and then to give a candid hearing to those whom our conduct has offended. The government must not hesitate. The western people will not be trifled with." The loss of their friendship would invite the loss of the territory forever.

Finally Brown addressed the members of Congress: "From you, assembled Representatives, do we demand that you would seize the happy moment for securing the possession of America to our posterity. . . . Give us not room to question your courage in a case where courage is truly a virtue, or to doubt your wisdom when the motives to decide your conduct are so obvious and forcible. *The iron is now hot;* command us to rise as one man and *strike!*"

This pamphlet was the most startling piece of propaganda issued by the Federalists during Jefferson's administration. Its revelation of hostile designs against the United States seemed not idle gossip but actual fact; the monster had at last bared his fangs. New edge was given to that keen and anxious solicitude felt for the honor and prosperity of the young nation. The New York *Evening Post* from January 24 to January 28 reprinted and analyzed much of "this interesting production, believing that if anything can arouse the government and the people of this country to a proper sense of the dangers which menace their peace from the magnificent and alarming projects of a towering, ambitious foreigner, it will be the perusal of this pamphlet. . . . It is eloquent and ingenious. That the views of the writer are comprehensive and the maxims of policy which he inculcates just and dignified, few American readers will be disposed to deny."

Other Federalist papers echoed the *Evening Post*. The Philadelphia *Gazette of the United States*, while admitting the gravity of the charges, stated: "We think the memorial is not genuine because it purports to have been published before the cession of Louisiana to France,—a period of fifteen months distant from the publication in this country, during which time, important as it is to us, we have heard nothing of it."

The Philadelphia *Aurora*, long the mouthpiece of Jeffersonian democracy, ranted against the pamphlet, snooped into the publisher's office to discover the author, and churned the waters of discussion into a muddy froth. Denouncing the memorial as a forgery, the *Aurora* on January 26 declared: "The artfulness of the design is, however, inferior to the execution, and though it might deceive the uninformed for a few hours, it could not impose on the discerning and intelligent a single moment. . . . This work we pronounce to be an impudent and gross fabrication." For a month the pamphlet was a daily subject of denunciation. On the 28th the editor wrote:

The Washington *Federalist* and Alexander Hamilton's *Evening Post* have both seized on this reputed memoir as a precious morceau in the present dearth of matter on which to found new tales of alarm. . . . The object of this pamphlet we believe to be to plunge this country into a war with France and Spain. . . . The sentiments of the translator (or writer) of the pamphlet completely coincide with those of the wicked amongst the editors of the Federalist prints. . . . We conclude that this pamphlet was to play a great part in the attempt to produce a war, for after all our Federal ranting in and out of Congress about the dangers from the French when in Louisiana, out comes a Frenchman to make them appear more terrific.

From Federalist as well as from Democratic editors came reiterated requests for the name of the American author. Brown on January 26 issued the following equivocal statement:

The translator cannot help thinking that his word deserves peculiar credit in a case where vanity would naturally have tempted him, if conscience or safety had been disregarded, to assume the whole merit of these reflections to himself, and he does not hold himself highly obliged to those who have doubted his word. The cause in which he has taken up the pen is not such as to make him studious of concealment; and he should think himself entitled to immortal honor, should he prove, by this humble and accidental means, to have influenced the public opinions and conduct in the smallest degree on this important occasion.

The *Aurora*, seizing upon this statement as proof of deceptive, cheating tricks by the opposition, on February 2 stated:

The rank literary character who translated! the Counselor of State's memoir has made such a left-handed defense that some of Coleman's apologies or the [Boston] *Palladium's* doubts must be brought in to keep himself and his lucubration afloat. He in a part of his defense tells us that his reasons for believing the memoir to be genuine were that the writer betrayed great vanity and indiscreet loquacity! two reasons the most convincing, to be sure. Vanity in a Counselor of State's address to Bonaparte looks well at a distance, but how there could be found indiscreet loquacity in a work intended for the consul, and which was to be private, as all memoirs necessarily are, we cannot comprehend. Another pamphlet explaining away all these trifles would—sell.

On February 10 the *Aurora* pointed to Brown as the author, but the evidence was inconclusive because the authorship was well masked. Two days later the paper returned to the hunt: "Who is the translator? . . . If the translator is a distinguished literary character and of high rank, why does he conceal himself when a question has arisen as to the genuineness of the memoir? and above all how could he dare to recommend hostilities from the contents of a work which he is unable or unwilling to say is not a forgery. We would recommend that he 'strike while the iron is hot.' Let him be known that he may be applauded or branded with infamy."

On February 18 Brown penned an "Advertisement" to the second, abridged edition of the pamphlet; he refused to identify himself, but he insisted upon speaking further about the course of events:

The editor withholds his name on this occasion merely because no name can give a just title to that audience which his arguments may fail to attain. Conscious of no sinister or factious views, he will cheerfully encounter, if necessary, all that the adverse zeal or clashing interests of others may suggest against him, and assumes no merit with those who approve, since he merely repeats what is to be heard in all public places, and urges considerations already familiar to the best part of his countrymen.

The measures being pursued by Congress were little to Brown's liking. A resolution appropriating two million dollars "to defray any expenses which may be incurred in relation to the intercourse between the United States and foreign nations" was approved by a special committee appointed on January 12, 1803. This committee reported that the fund was to facilitate negotiation with the French and Spanish governments relative to the purchase of New Orleans and the provinces of West and East Florida. Recognizing the importance of this territory to the future expansion of the American people as well as to the immediate safeguard of American shipping, the committee preferred to have those domains acquired through purchase rather than through war. If war comes, "foreign powers will be convinced that it is not a war of aggrandizement on our part. . . . Our measures will stand justified, not only to ourselves and our country, but to the world."

Brown and his Federalist friends feared that the usual dilatory methods of statecraft would be followed, the very methods he had inveighed against. A commission would be sent to Europe, and after delays involving impertinent treatment of our envoys, the Americans would return without having accomplished their aims. Brown anticipated appeasement and a sellout. James Monroe had been appointed to join with Robert Livingston, resident minister in Paris, in attempting negotiations with Bonaparte for the acquisition of New Orleans. Although appointed in January, Monroe did not leave until March. The Federalist newspapers abused Monroe's embassy, so that the *Aurora* had occasion to remark on February 22, 1803: "The talk about the expense of sending Mr. Monroe to France is solely the child of infuriate resentment to the government. All the Federal prints have expressed their dislike of the mission; they have not candor enough to acknowledge that it is because they dread a removal of differences, but tell us the measure will be attended with expense. Yet at the moment they wish to retain in the treasury a few thousand dollars, which too are expended to preserve peace, they voluntarily offer to appropriate five million to bring on a war!"

Brown's contribution to the argument was a fifty-seven-page pamphlet, *Monroe's Embassy, or, The Conduct of the Government in Relation to our Claims to the Navigation of the Mississippi*, published on March

3, 1803, and sold for twenty-five cents. This essay
stingingly rebuked Jefferson for employing dilatory
tactics when the public believed that the acquisition of
the Spanish province was at once "easy, desirable,
necessary, and just." War would be the cheapest means
of gaining the territory, and taxes for defraying a
military expedition would be paid willingly. "Why
should we consent to buy?" asked Brown. "Why divert
our revenue to channels from which it will never
return? Why cast millions into the coffers of strangers?" This money, he maintained, might construct
roads and harbors, and even be used to improve political relations with the Indians. He suggested further
that a compact be made with England which could
seal up French vessels in European harbors and prevent
troops from sailing to Louisiana. "Fate has manifestly
decreed," he wrote, "that America must belong to the
English name and race." He derided talk about expense and danger, because the future cries for action:
"The whole of our territory, however immense it
appears, will inevitably be occupied in thirty or forty
years. The possession of the mouth of the river, now
so easy and indispensable to our tranquillity and happiness, will, when occupied by the French, be acquired
with difficulty and at the price of a doubtful and dangerous war."

On March 10 Pichon, Chargé d'Affaires at Washington, wrote to the Governor of Louisiana that France,
as owner of the territory, was demanding that the port
be opened. Six days later France's ownership was pub-
licly avowed; hence, when Monroe sailed to Europe,
comment died down. In due season came the happy

news of successful negotiations whereby the Louisiana Territory and West Florida were purchased for fifteen million dollars.

Brown wrote two other political tracts, and it is possible that, at the behest of his brothers and other shipping men in Philadelphia, he became an anonymous penman of the Federalists in Philadelphia.

In 1806 Brown seemed unable to contain his wrath at Jefferson's management of international affairs. Because the navy was stuck in the mud in the Delaware River, merchantmen were denied safe conduct through seas infested with pirates and hostile men-of-war. Brown had seen his importing firm sink slowly under repeated blows. Although the President's maritime policy was not solely responsible for the bankruptcy of the Brown brothers' business, sufficient basis for the assumption was found. Two specific incidents goaded Brown: the signing of a treaty with England on December 31, 1806, and the agitation over the searching of the *Chesapeake* on June 22, 1807. Brown decided to let the public have the truth in an eighty-six-page pamphlet, *The British Treaty of Commerce and Navigation.* This essay analyzed the Jay Treaty of 1794 and the Treaty of 1806 for the purpose of showing that the former, although denounced by the Jeffersonians as a betrayal of the United States, was superior to the latter. The new document paralleled the old one in many of its provisions, but admitted stipulations damaging to the United States. The Mississippi River was opened equally to ships of both nations, but the St. Lawrence River remained restricted territory to Americans. Other restrictions worked hardship on

American commerce. Had a person acquainted with international trade been President, such evils would not have been tolerated. The whole point was that Jefferson, who sneered at Washington's treaty-making, had demonstrated complete ineptitude for negotiating with foreign countries. The discussion of the searching of the *Chesapeake* reflected Federalist Party thinking. The argument was that seamen hazard their lives for high wages, and that a neutral nation is not compromised by a search for men any more than by a search for contraband. Impressment should not cause excitement: "If an American be impressed, it is probably from mistake, and he suffers a misfortune incident to his profession."

In January, 1809, Brown published a ninety-seven-page pamphlet, signed C. B. B., and entitled *An Address to the Congress of the United States, on the Utility and Justice of Restrictions upon Foreign Commerce: With Reflections on Foreign Trade in General, and the Future Prospects of America*. Of the many pamphlets issued during the years of the Embargo, none, probably, analyzed more fairly and more completely all aspects of the problem than this essay. He wrote as a citizen distressed at an unwise policy. He did not call names as in 1807, nor did he express the slightest resentment against the leaders of either party or of France and England. Insisting that all nations are governed by self-interest, he traced the differences between Europe and America to their source, and gave proper perspective to the controversy. He explained the American reasons for the initiation of the Embargo, and showed why the measure had failed of success. He demonstrated "that all restrictions upon foreign commerce, whether as a precaution against future violences of foreign states, or as a mode of revenge and punishment for those already committed, or as a method of dissolving our connection with them altogether, are not warranted by justice, policy, or honor." A long section on the development of maritime law reached the conclusion that each nation conducts itself from a single principle—the promotion of its own advantage. Neutral rights exist only for those nations capable of asserting them; abrogation of rights brings a train of evils. The Embargo created so many unpleasant effects that they seemed quite beyond the reach of human calculation. America should return, Brown thought, to a system of international commerce, for it is only by trade that nations thrive. He expressed certainty that the causes of difficulty, originating in the European war, would soon end; trade would reopen on sea and on land. Ultimately France would be defeated, and old opportunities would revivify American commerce. His hope was that the United States would not go to war. Less than two months later, on March 13, the Embargo was repealed, only to be replaced by other forms of commercial restriction.

As a pamphleteer, Brown had a grasp of political and economic principles, of the history of international conflict, and especially of the much-debated problem of neutral rights.

Editor, Annalist, Geographer

THAT man is happy who keeps busy in congenial activities. Each man's mind chooses the vocation seemingly most suitable, but circumstances often waylay the individual and force him into hateful paths. While one brother succeeds or becomes rich because of his adjustment to his environment, another brother flounders in the wasteland of despair or batters himself to early death in a mental prison house seemingly of his own making. Charles Brockden Brown was one of those men who wanted to succeed in literature in a day when authorship seldom paid a writer's barest necessities. Newspaper editors were the only wielders of the quill likely to make a living from the written word. Preachers and lawyers and physicians seldom profited from their learned writings; usually they were delighted to have the printer's bill paid. A few textbook makers—Noah Webster, Jedidiah Morse, and Nicholas Pike—earned annual royalties in substantial amounts. Robert Treat Paine, Jr., the Boston poet, received large sums for his poems for a few years, but Paine was the exception proving the rule that authorship simply did not pay in the United States. Brown's entrance into mercantile pursuits had strong economic and family motivation. But that he could remain away from printer's ink was impossible. Once soiled with that black substance, a man cannot remove the stain or the ambition to influence the thoughts of his fellow men. The compelling intellectual ambition of Brown lay in the field of informational and didactic writing. To keep happy was to keep writing or at least disseminating useful information.

In aligning himself with John Conrad and Company, the Philadelphia printing and bookselling organization, Brown made the kind of tie which promised opportunity for remaining a literary man while earning a good salary. In September, 1803, he undertook the editing of *The Literary Magazine and American Register*. The title, like those of its predecessors, appealed to the nationalistic predilections of the American people, but the magazine itself lacked nativistic bias. Starting with the hope that original materials would fill the pages, Brown soon discovered that scissors and paste alone were reliable aids. In July, 1804, he wrote to John Blair Linn: "You will find but a single communication in this [June] number. All the rest of the original prose I have been obliged to supply myself, for which I am sorry, for the sake of the credit of the work as well as of my own ease. The whole original department of July, I have been obliged to spin out of my own brain. You will probably find it, of consequence, very dull."

Dull is not the word; the magazine lacked point, direction, intellectual elevation. It was a compendium of snippets on every kind of serious and startling information. The readers evidently were not expected to read more than five or ten minutes at a time, as if the magazine were a textbook in an elementary class in reading. Its pages contained a miscellany of essays, reviews, and a register of contemporary events. An appendix carried state papers, financial statements, tables of mortality, and similar official or statistical data. Much foreign material in translation came from French and German sources.

The only original narrative by Brown was "Memoirs of Carwin, the Biloquist," the promised continuation of *Wieland*. Twice publication of this story ceased, and each time readers requested additional chapters. In 1804 he refused to continue. Except for additions to "Sketches of a History of Carsol" and "Sketches of a History of the Carrils and Ormes," he abandoned fiction after 1804 or 1805. Unhappily the dispersal and destruction of his papers render impossible a knowledge of the reasons for this action. In the prospectus to the magazine he made the following quite amazing statement, denying merit to himself as an author:

I am far from wishing, however, that my readers should judge of my exertions by my former ones. I have written much, but take much blame to myself for something which I have written, and take no praise for anything. I should enjoy a larger share of my own respect at the present moment if nothing had ever flowed from my pen, the production of which could be traced to me. A variety of causes induces me to form such a wish, but I am principally influenced by the consideration that time can scarcely fail of enlarging and refining the powers of a man, while the world is sure to judge of his capacities and principles at fifty from what he has written at fifteen.

Brown bowed to popular demand in his magazine. He refused to permit politics and theology to sully its pages with controversy. He insisted upon a moral aim: "Everything that savors of indelicacy or licentiousness will be rigorously proscribed." He preferred the contents to be dull rather than naughty; he aimed to promote public and private virtue. He promised as a Christian to champion morality and religion and to recommend the practice of religious duties. His growing interests in annal writing, an occupation popularized by the new interest in native history, was thus explained:

He [the editor] will pay particular attention to the history of passing events. He will carefully compile the news, foreign and domestic, of the current month, and give in a concise and systematic order that intelligence which the common newspapers communicate in a vague and indiscriminate way. His works shall likewise be a repository for all those signal incidents in private life which mark the character of the age and excite the liveliest curiosity. . . . As a political annalist he will speculate freely on foreign transactions; but in his detail of domestic events he will confine himself, as strictly as possible, to the limits of a mere historian. There is nothing for which he has a deeper abhorrence than the intemperance of party, and his fundamental rule shall be to exclude from his pages all personal altercation and abuse.

The magazine circulated through the chain of Conrad shops from Philadelphia southward, and it seems to have been very successful. The Conrads, being of German stock, operated chiefly in communities with large German immigrant groups. This circumstance, as well as the growing popularity of German literature, led the editor to devote an increasing amount of space to biographical information about German authors. Accounts of inventions, natural disasters, and robberies provided grist for the average man's conversation mill. An essay on "Fame" correctly gauged public interest in such topics:

> Great misfortunes or great crises are inevitable roads to notoriety. In England and America where newspaper and periodical works fly about in such numbers and penetrate into even the remotest and obscurest corner, the history of a worthless individual whom nobody knew in his lifetime shall after his death be an object of curiosity to millions. One who died of famine and neglect in the darkest garret of the obscurest alley in London shall twelve months afterward be, in all his habits and concerns, intimately known to the inhabitants of Jamaica, Canada, Bengal, and Kentucky.

To these human-interest items, Brown joined enough information on agriculture, medicine, and law, as well as on the conventional literary topics, to keep the widest variety of readers contented. The editor's task, therefore, was not so much one of composing new tales or new moralizing essays as of translating, adapting, or excerpting from books and periodicals.

At the launching of the magazine, Brown's friends

in New York promised to contribute essays and poems. In April, 1804, the following reminder appeared in "Notes from the Editor": "The literary fraternity of New York, friends of the editor and of the editor's friends, are respectfully saluted and requested not to be unmindful in the midst of their professional engagements of their promises." Help came from John Blair Linn. John E. Hall, a youthful Baltimorean with literary aspirations, submitted essays, signed J. E. H., on the poetry of Anacreon.

Brown's favorite authors were Shakespeare, Cicero, and Milton. Throughout his works, there are frequent allusions to and verbal echoes of these writers. His long familiarity with the Puritan poet appears in an article in the *Literary Magazine* of October, 1803:

I have now in my hands an old copy of Milton, which at first belonged to my father. It is an old book, and few volumes have been oftener in my hands. I would not exchange it for an edition of the same work embellished by all the arts of the printer, the engraver, and the binder. . . . Milton is only inferior to the voice of inspiration. He is first among the poets who were not prophets. . . . I consider the relish for the poetry of Milton as a criterion of the taste and mental elevation of the reader. . . . I could fill a volume in speaking of Milton, so keen is my sensibility to his excellencies, so great is the instruction and pleasure which I have received from him. I have marked many of his passages in my almost worn-out copy. . . . To these I sometimes recur with satisfaction; they are mementos of former periods which have been passed in converse with the mighty bard, and of some hours of dejection which were lightened by his voice.

Late in 1806 after the death of John Conrad, the magazine was taken over by the printers Thomas and George Palmer who discontinued publication in December, 1807. Whether Brown remained editor during its last year is not known.

Among the tasks Brown completed for Conrad, in addition to the political pamphlets already mentioned, was a translation—"with occasional remarks"—of Volney's *A View of the Soil and Climate of the United States*. Brown spent the summer of 1804 in transcribing this work and in preparing footnotes of jeering rebuttal, such as "It is somewhat surprising that notions so crude and so generally exploded [as that of a prevailing wind bringing wisdom to one nation and stupidity to another] should be countenanced by our author." Brown took occasion to rebuke Americans for their absurd modes of eating and dress, for their intemperate use of spirituous liquors, and for their general recklessness in respect to their health. Among other data he noted: "The terror of lightning, which prevails greatly, especially among the female sex, is a genuine and formidable evil in the United States." In pointing out Volney's many errors and his abhorrence of Rousseau and his man of nature, Brown generously remarked: "Instead of reproaching him for the mistakes committed, we should grant him liberal applause for the truths he has attained." The editorial changes involved a shortening of sentences, the elimination of unnecessary epistolary connective devices, the alteration of thermometrical readings from the calculations of Reaumur to those of Fahrenheit, and the supplying of interesting notes explanatory of the text. Brown's reading in every branch of learning seems to have been as accurate as it was wide. The book was issued late in 1804.

On July 4, 1804, Brown had written to John Blair Linn the following gloomy lines:

As to my own particular condition and feelings, I cannot rejoice your heart by an agreeable intelligence. I have had less to boast of on the score of health than for some considerable time backward, and the world of business has been darkened by unusual vexations, disappointment, and embarrassments. I, however, endeavor to make the most of the small portion of good that falls to my lot, to think only on the brightest parts of the present scene, and to send out hope to explore the future.

Despite prospects clouded by illness and financial uncertainty, Brown and Elizabeth Linn were married in New York City on November 19, 1804, by the bride's father, the Reverend William Linn. In going outside the bounds of the Society of Friends for a mate, Brown violated the rules of his sect as well as the wishes of his parents. The Philadelphia Meeting passed a resolution of censure, a proceeding so common in Brown's day and family as to have lost any except ceremonial significance. Brown petitioned successfully for a right of membership. His name remained upon the books of the congregation until his death, and his body was interred in the old burial ground. The certificate of censure is as follows:

Charles Brockden Brown of this city who had by birth a right of membership in our Religious Society having accomplished his marriage by the assistance of an hireling minister to a person not in profession with us, it became our concern tenderly to treat with him on that account. But not appearing duly sensible of the impropriety of his conduct, we testify that we cannot consider him a member among us, yet desire that through submission to the operation of Truth he may be qualified to condemn his transgression to the satisfaction of this meeting and become united in religious fellowship with us.

Elizabeth Linn brought that marital comfort and felicity Brown had so long yearned for. Quietly she devoted her days and nights to the care of her enfeebled husband and to the rearing of a family of attractive children. On August 10, 1805, twin boys were born: Charles Brockden Brown, Jr., and William Linn Brown. Both survived into old age, and both played important roles in the business life of Philadelphia. On July 26, 1807, Eugene Linn Brown was born. Seventeen years later, on April 6, 1824, Poulson's *American Daily Advertiser* thus chronicled his death:

The recently deceased Mr. Eugene L. Brown, son of the celebrated Charles Brockden Brown, was a youth of uncommon talents and promise. By his death our country has been disappointed in the expectations that were reasonably indulged in anticipation of the maturity of a sound mind cultivated with great application and strengthened by extensive acquirements. He possessed force of mind very seldom met with even at a more advanced age; and his conversation, studies, and inclinations marked him a sound, ingenious scholar, and bid fair in mature life to render him a distinguished literary character. A consumption of the lungs caused his dissolution, which toward the close of his career was anticipated with the reasoning and composure of a sage.

A daughter, Mary Brown, also was born to the couple, but further details of her life beyond a single mention in a will have not been found.

Charles and Elizabeth Brown had established themselves in the house at 74, now 124, South Eleventh Street, on the west side below Chestnut Street. After Brown's death, Mrs. Brown conducted a boarding house, first at this address and later at other places. Her subsequent career is unknown, beyond the fact that she died on August 31, 1834.

On the death of Linn, Brown wrote a memoir as a preface for an edition of Linn's *Valerian*. The biography is indefinite and moralizing. The one man capable of leaving a precise record of the features, moods, and ambitions of Linn wrote an essay consisting of a few generalizations.

Dunlap had fallen upon hard days. The theater slipped out of his hands, his draper's shop no longer was profitable, and plays were not saleable. He returned of necessity to his first love, painting, and became an itinerant portrait maker. A note to Brown about his plight in 1805 brought an instantaneous response. Dunlap evidently planned to sell an edition of his plays to Conrad, but the financial stringency resulting from the Embargo dimmed hope of success. Yet, desirous of buoying his friend, even as he himself had been cheered in the past, Brown added the following account of his own circumstances as a married man:

As to myself, my friend, you judge rightly when you think me situated happily; my present way of life is in every respect to my mind. There is nothing to disturb my felicity but the sense of the uncertainty and instability that sticks to everything human. I cannot be happier than I am. Every change, therefore, must be for the worse. My business, if I may so call it, is altogether pleasurable, and, such as it is, it occupies not one fourth of my time. My companion is all that an husband can wish for, and, in short, as to my own personal situation I have nothing to wish but that it may last.

Later, on November 6, Brown wrote Dunlap apologizing for failing, as in the past, to keep up a correspondence. His excuse was a husband's apprehension lest all not go well during Mrs. Brown's confinement:

My domestic felicities were so great that I shuddered at the approach of an event by which they were endangered. The event came and instead of depriving me of an adored wife has added two lovely children to my store. They are sons, counterparts of each other, with all their members and faculties complete, and enjoying as far as we can judge, after two months' trial of life and its perils, the admirable constitution of their mother. Do not you congratulate me on this event?

In January, 1806, Dunlap spent two weeks in the Brown home while painting portraits of notable Philadelphians. The two friends went over old plans as they played backgammon, but they formed no new ones. Brown's course was now laid out for his few remaining years. On January 14 Dunlap and Brown were among the guests at a dinner given by Conrad. Others present included Thomas Green Fessenden, the poet and mechanical genius; Joseph Dennie, editor of the *Port Folio;* John Vaughan, a member of the American Philosophical Society; and Dr. Nathaniel Chapman, a Philadelphia surgeon. Brown divulged the information that Armitt was distressed over the danger to a loaded, outbound vessel ice-locked in the Delaware. He also told numerous anecdotes about his editorial trials. One concerned an impudent author who had requested that a book of travels be praised in a review. Another concerned the squabble over the review of John Davis' *Travels*, a work in which Brown was mentioned. Later, when Dunlap returned in March and in April for further visits, the friends enjoyed a repetition of the pleasures experienced years earlier when Brown made Perth Amboy a regular stopping place on journeys between Philadelphia and New York.

In June, 1806, Brown again made a trip to New York and up the Hudson to regain strength. On the boat from New York to Albany he made the acquaintance of the youthful actor John Howard Payne, then on his way to enter Union College. Brown took an affectionate, fatherly interest in the lad, and after returning home from his pleasant visit with Mrs. Brown's sisters, he wrote on August 25, 1806, a friendly letter of counsel to Payne. On February 22, 1809, another letter acknowledged a copy of the *Boston Mirror*, Payne's magazine devoted to the drama, and again evinced "earnest regard" for the actor.

In 1806 Brown entered an agreement with the Conrads to produce *The American Register or General Repository of History, Politics, and Science.* He prepared five semiannual volumes before his fatal illness.

In a sense the *Register* was a continuation of the statistical portion of the *Literary Magazine*. Important intelligence printed in state papers, books, magazines, and newspapers formed the basis for a chronology and for an analytical interpretation of events in Europe and America. Brown was thus the first American to prepare a historical digest based upon contemporary documents and designed to clarify important events at home and abroad. Hezekiah Niles began his famous *Weekly Register* shortly after Brown's death, and may have derived his editorial principles from the pioneer compilation. In some 35,000 words in the first volume, Brown gave an abstract of laws and public acts passed by Congress between December, 1805, and April 21, 1806; a catalogue and general review of books published in England and the United States in the year 1806; a chronicle of memorable occurrences for 1806-1807; British and foreign intelligence, chiefly scientific; American and foreign state papers; miscellaneous articles about nations and persons; an American register of deaths; and a few selected poems extracted from newspapers. Volume I comprises 526 pages, and the four other volumes are approximately the same length and similar in content.

This historical writing is notable for its attempt to secure all available evidence, its fair presentation of all sides, and its effort to avoid bias. Its weakness lies in its failure to depict scenes graphically or to detail events in the order of their occurrence. Again the generalizer and moralizer is at work. Yet historical insight, as well as frequent felicitous phrases, makes the *Register* even now a valuable source book on events between 1806 and

1809. The review of American literature in 1806 and 1807 gives an excellent first-hand account of the difficulties faced by writers in those years.

The *Register* shows little evidence of being hack work; the task was completed conscientiously in the old-school historical manner by a writer still anxious to demonstrate his usefulness to his country as a literary man. A nation's thinking is as correct as its information; Brown tried to supply unbiased, full information. That he succeeded in so tumultuous a time as the close of Jefferson's administration testifies to his high purpose and clear vision. However humble this labor was by comparison with the more startling novels of terror, Brown believed that he was serving his country better by giving truthful information than by titillating its nerves with fictitious tales.

Blow after blow began to fall upon Brown after 1806. He undertook a journey for his health in the full knowledge that his cough might develop into a fatal consumption. On April 6, 1807, his sister, Elizabeth Armitt Brown Horner, died in childbirth. Joseph Armitt Brown, the successful merchant, died in Flushing, Holland, on October 29, 1807. And on January 8, 1808, the father of Mrs. Brown passed away. The leaves were falling fast, and the early frost had touched Brown himself. In the midst of multiplied sorrows came also the joys of parenthood. Life and death in its endless procession warned Brown to count his days. Each new attack of coughing seemed no worse than its predecessor, yet the clapper on the bell was swinging in an ever increasing arc, ready soon to knell the end.

Brown's ambition to leave a heroic monument of his

intellectual activity never wavered as a result of illness. While daily grinding the grist for the *Register*, he also laid together notes for *A System of General Geography*, a proposed two-volume work which would embrace a topographical, statistical, and descriptive survey of the Earth, as well as an account of the Earth as a planetary body in the solar system. The first volume would survey the United States; the second, the remainder of the world. Much of this project was completed; on June 13, 1811, Mrs. Brown entered a contract with Paul Allen to oversee its publication. C. and A. Conrad willingly agreed to publish the work, but something went askew with the plans. The manuscript has been lost, and only the prospectus survives as evidence of Brown's labors.

In the summer of 1809 he made the last of the annual journeys in search of health. He left reluctantly, as if fearing that he would not return alive. In a letter to a sister-in-law he complained of homesickness, of depressed spirits continually hovering on the brink of dejection, and of illness. "When," he asked, "have I known that lightness and vivacity of mind which the divine flow of health, even in calamity, produces in some men? . . . Never: scarcely ever: not longer than an half hour at a time since I have called myself man."

He traveled to Perth Amboy, Belleville, and Passaic Falls, New Jersey. "The weather was insupportably hot," he observed, "and the fatigue of even those short walks, which curiosity required, added to my inharmonious feelings, contributed to make the journey rather unprofitable. Glittering waterfalls are but dim, and hanging rocks hardly more interesting than a sand moor when viewed with misty eyes and aching brows."

At Hoboken he gazed across the river to New York City; here he conjured up dreams of what might have been and thoughts of what actually happened when he had cast his lot with the growing city on Manhattan Island nearly fifteen years earlier. Here he found that comfort which nature never afforded him: "Till here I could not find books, which have with me great efficacy in beguiling body of its pains and thoughts of their melancholy, in relieving head and heart of their aches." His gloom deepened as he meditated upon "death, funeral, interment," events possible in the three days since he parted from home. He was tempted to return home immediately. "I am afraid," he wrote, "when the next horn sounds I shall find the temptation irresistible."

At his home in Philadelphia on November 10, 1809, Brown suffered a violent pain in his side. In accordance with the medical practice of that day, he was bled and put to bed. It was expected that he would be well within a few days. But he never left his bed. Daily he grew feebler, complained of gastric pains, and manifested symptoms of advanced tuberculosis. Expectoration of blood grew more frequent; now it was realized that he had done wrong to minimize these occurrences in the past two years. Plans were made for a sea voyage to England, where his brother James had gone to continue the business activities of Joseph. During his illness Charles never expressed sentiments of impatience or complaint. Covertly he gave instructions to his family friends: "You must do so and so when I am absent." On February 19, 1810, a change for the worse appeared.

In perfect possession of his faculties until the end, he bade farewell to his family. In his thirty-ninth year on February 22, 1810, he breathed his last.

The following obituary notice appeared in Poulson's *American Daily Advertiser* on February 27 and in the *United States Gazette* a day later:

DIED, In this city . . . of pulmonary consumption, Charles Brockden Brown, editor of the semiannual register. . . . He died in the enjoyment of his mental faculties, a Christian, full of the hope of immortality, at peace with himself and with all mankind.

The manners of the deceased were mild and un-affected—his attachment to his friends ardent and sincere—his knowledge extensive—and his criticisms were generally admitted to be acute, liberal, and profound—and if in early life he indulged in speculative theories and opinions, it was to be ascribed to the versatile exuberance of a brilliant imagination, to the unwearied inquisitiveness of a rich and active mind, and to that never-failing propensity to scrutiny and investigation, consequent on a disposition to admit nothing on trust when in search of truth. He was blessed by nature with the most facile capacity for the acquirement of knowledge, and having received a liberal education which he greatly improved by study and research, and possessing at the same time a laudable but modest ambition for the acquirement of literary fame, together with the most copious command of language and the happy art of communicating his thoughts with perspicuity and force, he seemed destined to become one of the brightest ornaments of his country.

He lived in innocent but not inactive seclusion from the world, being wholly devoted to literary pursuits, to a beloved family, and to the society of a few select friends, to whom he devoted himself by the most amiable and disinterested attentions, by his overflowing affability, and by the instructiveness of his unassuming conversations. Few perhaps ever exceeded him in the varied richness and fertility of his colloquial powers, and by few has he been surpassed in the candor with which he examined the opinions and defects of others.

As the end came, in the realization that he had run his brief course in the strange way prescribed by his peculiar physical and psychological structure, Brown may have thought of the words he penned in *Arthur Mervyn:* "Death is the inevitable and universal lot. When or how it comes is of little moment. To stand when so many thousands are falling around me is not to be expected. I have acted an humble and obscure part in the world, and my career has been short; but I murmur not at the decree that makes it so."

Bibliography

Books and Pamphlets by Charles Brockden Brown

Alcuin; A Dialogue. New York, 1798.
Reprinted in type facsimile, with an introduction by LeRoy Elwood Kimball, New York, 1935.

Wieland; or, The Transformation. An American Tale. New York, 1798.
Reprinted New York and London, 1811; London, 1822; Boston, 1827; New York, 1846; Philadelphia, 1857, 1887, 1889; and, with an introduction by Fred Lewis Pattee, New York, 1926. A French translation apparently appeared in 1800 and another as *Wieland, ou la voix mystérieuse*, Paris, 1841. A German translation appeared before 1858, but a copy has not been located.

Ormond; or, The Secret Witness. New York, 1799.
Reprinted London, 1800; Boston, 1827; London, 1839; New York, 1846; Philadelphia, 1857, 1887; and, with an introduction by Ernest Marchand, New York, 1937.

Arthur Mervyn; or, Memoirs of the Year 1793. Two volumes. [First Part], Philadelphia, 1799. Second Part, New York, 1800.
Reprinted in three volumes, London, 1803; in two volumes, Boston, 1827; Philadelphia, 1857, 1883, 1887, 1889. A German translation appeared in Leipzig about 1858.

Edgar Huntly; or, Memoirs of a Sleep-Walker. Three volumes. Philadelphia, 1799. "The Death of Cicero" is included in Volume III.
Reprinted Philadelphia, 1801; London, 1803; Boston, 1827; London, 1831, 1842, 1847, 1857; Philadelphia, 1857, 1887; and, with an introduction by David Lee Clark, New York, 1928. A German translation appeared in Leipzig before 1858.

Clara Howard; in a Series of Letters. Philadelphia, 1801.
Reprinted as *Philip Stanley; or, The Enthusiasm of Love.* Two volumes. London, 1807. Reprinted as *Clara Howard; or, The Enthusiasm of Love*, Boston, 1827; Philadelphia, 1857, 1887.

Bibliography

Jane Talbot, A Novel. Philadelphia, 1801.
   Reprinted in two volumes, London, 1804. In one volume, Boston, 1827; Philadelphia, 1857, 1887.

An Address to the Government of the United States of America: on the Cession of Louisiana to the French; and on the Late Breach of Treaty by the Spaniards: Including the Translation of a Memorial, on the War of St. Domingo, and Cession of the Mississippi to France. Drawn up by a French Counsellor of State. Philadelphia, 1803.
   Reprinted in an abridged version, Philadelphia, 1803, and as *Interesting Account of the Project of France Respecting Louisiana*, Martinsburg [West Virginia], 1803.

Monroe's Embassy; or, The Conduct of the Government in Relation to Our Claims to the Navigation of the Mississippi. Philadelphia, 1803.

A View of the Soil and Climate of the United States of America: With Supplementary Remarks upon Florida; on the French Colonies on the Mississippi and Ohio, and in Canada; and on the Aboriginal Tribes of America. By C. F. Volney. Translated, with Occasional Remarks, by C. B. Brown. Philadelphia, 1804.
   A translation of *Tableau du Climat et du Sol des États-Unis* by Constantin François de Chasseboeuf, Comte de Volney.

The British Treaty of Commerce and Navigation, Concluded December 31, 1806. Philadelphia, 1807.
   Reprinted as *The British Treaty. With an Appendix of State Papers*. London, 1808.

An Address to the Congress of the United States, on the Utility and Justice of Restrictions upon Foreign Commerce. With Reflections on Foreign Trade in General, and the Future Prospects of America. Philadelphia, 1809.

Carwin, The Biloquist, and Other American Tales and Pieces. Three volumes. London, 1802.
   Contains "Carwin, the Biloquist," "Stephen Calvert," "Jessica," and "The Scribbler."

The Novels of Charles Brockden Brown. Seven volumes. Boston, 1827.
   Reprinted in six volumes, Philadelphia, 1857, 1887.

Bibliography

*The Rhapsodist and Other Uncollected Writings of Charles Brock-
    den Brown.* Edited, with an introduction, by Harry R. Warfel.
    New York, 1943.
    Contains "The Rhapsodist," "The Man at Home," "A Series
    of Original Letters," "Advertisement for 'Sky-Walk,'" "An
    Extract from 'Sky-Walk,'" and "Walstein's School of History."

Sources

THE chief source of biographical information concerning Charles
Brockden Brown is William Dunlap's *The Life of Charles Brockden Brown: together with Selections from the Rarest of His Printed
Works, from His Original Letters, and from His Manuscripts before Unpublished* (Philadelphia, 1815). This two-volume work was
originally undertaken by Paul Allen at the request of Brown's
family, but, after "the selections for the first volume had been
made and printed," the task was relinquished to Dunlap. Preserved
in the *Life* are passages from the diaries, eighteen letters, and
other useful autobiographical writings, the manuscripts of which
have disappeared. Unhappily the work is shoddy, inaccurate, in-
complete, and quite unworthy of the talents of Dunlap or Brown.
An abridged English edition appeared as *Memoirs of Charles Brockden Brown* (London, 1822).

Dunlap prepared three other works in which additional biographical details and a few letters appear: *A History of the American Theatre* (New York, 1832), *A History of the Rise and Progress
of the Arts of Design in the United States* (New York, 1834), and
"Diary of William Dunlap" in *Collections of the New York Historical Society*, LXII-LXIV. The best character analysis of Brown
by a contemporary is in John Bernard's *Retrospections of America*
(New York, 1887). John Davis' *Travels of Four Years and a Half
in the United States* (London, 1803) recounts a conversation.

Brown's letters and manuscripts have almost entirely disappeared.
The Historical Society of Pennsylvania owns a collection of note-
books kept by members of the Brown family, several letters by
Brown, a portion of a manuscript version of *Alcuin*, and an unpublished fragment of a tale. Annie Russell Marble in *Heralds*

of *American Literature* (Chicago, 1907) has printed some of this material. Individual letters are owned by the Harvard College Library, Library of Congress, New York Public Library, Ridgway Branch of the Philadelphia Library Company, Friends Historical Library at Swarthmore College, and the Quaker Collection at Haverford College. The unpublished diaries of Elihu Hubbard Smith, which are now on deposit in the Yale University Library, define Brown's whereabouts from 1794 to 1798 and contain copies of several of Smith's letters to Brown. Ernest Marchand in *Ormond* (New York, 1937) has printed a letter by Brown of July 8, 1802, when the novelist was in New York writing half a dozen book reviews for the *American Review*. William Peden printed a letter from Brown to Jefferson of December 25, 1798, in "Thomas Jefferson and Charles Brockden Brown," *Maryland Quarterly*, II (1944), 65-68.

Family background and genealogy are found in J. Smith Fuhey and Gilbert Cope's *History of Chester County, Pennsylvania* (Philadelphia, 1881; p. 488); J. M. Hoppin's *Memoir of Henry Armitt Brown, together with Four Historical Orations* (Philadelphia, 1880), particularly "The Settlement of Burlington, New Jersey," on pages 280-81; and David Lee Clark's forty-nine-page abstract of an undeposited and unavailable Columbia University dissertation, "Charles Brockden Brown: A Critical Biography" (New York, 1923). Clark claims to have seen Brown's diaries and correspondence once owned by William Linn Brown, but the present location of this material has not been revealed.

The land and probate records of Philadelphia, preserved in the Philadelphia City Hall, throw light on the business activities of the Brown family. The Badcock-Lisle-Brockden connection is found in deed book I, 1: 131-35. Deed book GWR 18: 509 names on October 8, 1827, Brown's three children then living: William, Charles, and Mary.

A thorough search in the files of contemporaneous newspapers brought to light a few new biographical facts, some hitherto unreported reviews, and the controversies raging around Brown's political pamphlets. These items are located in the text of this biography. From publishers' and booksellers' advertisements in newspapers came precise dates of publication of the novels and magazines; for example, the Philadelphia *Aurora* of May 21, 1799, contains the first announcement of the first volume of *Arthur Mervyn*, and the Washington, D. C., *Universal Gazette* of July 2, 1801, states that *Clara Howard* is "just published."

The fullest bibliographies of works by and about Brown are in *The Cambridge History of American Literature* (New York, 1917), I, 527-29; W. F. Taylor's *History of American Letters* (New York, 1936), 491-92; and *Literary History of the United States* (New York, 1948), III, 417-19. Editions of Brown's novels published in London by the Minerva Press are given in Dorothy Blakey's *The Minerva Press, 1790-1820* (London, 1929). Ernest Marchand's edition of *Ormond* (New York, 1937) contains an annotated selected bibliography.

Index

Index

Index

Index

Index

Index

Psychology in Brown's fiction, 5, 8, 107, 129, 154, 161, 193, 197

QUAKERS, 7, 14-15, 17, 18-20, 26-27, 227

RADCLIFFE, Anne, 109, 129, 138, 155-156

Religion as a theme in Brown's novels, 101, 130-131, 136, 198-200

"Rhapsodist, The," by C. B. Brown, 33-35, 37

"Rights of Women, The," by C. B. Brown, 92

Riley, 98

Rochefoucauld, 108

Rogers, Moses, 98

Roulet, M., 73, 98

Rousseau, Jean Jacques, 27, 41, 63, 226

Rumford, Count, 76

Rush, Dr. Benjamin, 5, 41, 76, 107, 167, 173

Russian Discoveries, by William Coxe, 71

SALCEDO, 205

Scandella, Dr. Joseph, 118-121, 144

Schiller, 110, 170

Scott, Job, 17

Scott, Sir Walter, 155

Searson, John, 172

"Series of Original Letters, A," by C. B. Brown, 92, 93-94, 128

Shakers, 195

Shakespeare, William, 9, 225

Shelley, Percy Bysshe, 140

Simpson, Solomon, 99

Sketches of a History of Carsol, by C. B. Brown, 70-72, 76, 222

Sketches of the History of the Carrils and Ormes, by C. B. Brown, 72-73, 222

Sky-Walk, by C. B. Brown, 88-91, 92, 100, 128

"Sleepless Man of Madrid, History of the," 75

Smith, Elihu Hubbard, 40-49, 50-52, 55-56, 70-76, 78-79, 80-82, 86, 87, 88, 97, 99, 100, 116-122, 126, 144, 165, 170, 187

Smith, Samuel Harrison, 139

Society for the Attainment of Useful Knowledge, 35

"Song of Roland," 54

Southey, Robert, 174

Spectator, New York, 110, 122, 172

Spectator, The, by Addison and Steele, 33

Spy, The, by James Fenimore Cooper, 4, 155

State Gazette of North Carolina, Edenton, 32

Steele, Sir Richard, 33

Stephen Calvert, Memoirs of, by C. B. Brown, 115, 126

Index